MW01193941

Advance praise for *How to Be a Grown Up*

"As a therapist, I see young adults every day who have been taught everything in school except the skills, habits, and wisdom they need to navigate their lives. This is an absolute must-read for every person in their twenties!"

—**Lori Gottlieb**, *New York Times* bestselling author of *Maybe You Should Talk to Someone*

"Raffi Grinberg is a born teacher with a keen eye for what his students most need to know and with a talent for explaining even complex ideas about finance, love, and critical thinking in a way that is clear, compelling, and fun. I wish all twentysomethings could take his class, and now, with *How to Be a Grown Up*, they can."

—**Jonathan Haidt**, *New York Times* bestselling author of *The Anxious Generation* and co-author of *The Coddling of the American Mind*

"Readable, practical, and relatable, *How to Be a Grown Up* is the primer that every young adult could use. I wish I'd had this book when I was in my twenties!"

—**Meg Jay**, PhD, bestselling author of *The Defining Decade* and *The Twenty-something Treatment*

"Raffi Grinberg deftly addresses the questions that every young person asks but that nobody ever answers. *How to Be a Grown Up* is a farsighted yet down-to-earth guide that transforms the daunting task of adulting into an achievable set of skills."

—**Daniel H. Pink**, #1 *New York Times* bestselling author of *The Power of Regret*, *Drive*, and *To Sell Is Human*

"*How to Be a Grown Up* is a wonderful survival guide for navigating the often-overlooked challenges of adulthood. Raffi offers practical advice, humor, and lessons designed to help readers avoid a quarter-life crisis and thrive in the real world."

—**Charles Duhigg**, *New York Times* bestselling author of *Supercommunicators* and *The Power of Habit*

"Today's education system is an ancient relic. *How to Be a Grown Up* is the solution to this problem—a fun and incredibly practical guide through all the critical lessons missing from today's schooling, full of brilliant analogies that make the book both addictive and memorable."

—**Tim Urban**, writer at WaitButWhy.com and bestselling author of *What's Our Problem?*

How to Be a Grown Up

The 14 Essential Skills You Didn't Know You Needed (Until Just Now)

Raffi Grinberg

CHRONICLE PRISM

To Charlotte—
we grew into adults together

Contents

INTRODUCTION

Skill #1 – FIND YOUR PURPOSES (RIGHT NOW) 9

I. Mental Skills

Skill #2 – FACE REJECTION 24
Skill #3 – THINK CRITICALLY 35
Skill #4 – REFRAME AUTOMATIC THOUGHTS 43

II. Financial Skills

Skill #5 – BUILD CREDIT 62
Skill #6 – INVEST YOUR MONEY 83
Skill #7 – GET INSURANCE AND PAY TAXES 118
Skill #8 – STICK TO A BUDGET 157

III. Relationship Skills

Skill #9 – HAVE GOOD CONVERSATIONS 174
Skill #10 – FIND FRIENDS (AND LOVE) 187
Skill #11 – EVOLVE WITH YOUR PARENTS 205

IV. Career Skills

Skill #12 – ACE YOUR FIRST JOB 220
Skill #13 – LAUNCH YOUR CAREER 234

CONCLUSION

Skill #14 – LIVE ON PURPOSE 255

RECOMMENDED READING AND VIEWING 264
ACKNOWLEDGMENTS 265
CONTACT 268
ABOUT THE AUTHOR 269

[INTRODUCTION]

Skill #1

FIND YOUR PURPOSES (RIGHT NOW)

Congratulations! You may have just finished college, or high school, or moved out of your parents' house, and you are beginning your life as an adult.

And you're beginning to realize that the vast majority of what you learned in high school and college has no practical relevance to your life.

Even worse: There are many things you *do* need to know about adult life, and none of them were taught to you.

Why I wrote this book

I was in your shoes. Upon graduating college, I was beginning a job that I wasn't sure I wanted. I still didn't know what my career should be, and my degree in theoretical math wasn't going to help. I didn't know how to get health insurance, I didn't have a credit card, and I wasn't saving for retirement (I didn't know that was even a thing). I was in a happy relationship but unsure of when I wanted to get married, let alone have kids. I didn't really know how to be a good partner. I didn't know how to maintain a good relationship with my parents now that our parent-child dynamic had changed. And now that I wasn't chasing grades, I didn't know what the goal was anymore. I didn't know how to be happy.

That was just the tip of the iceberg. The following years would bring new adulting challenges: career surprises, financial mishaps (including nearly going broke), moves, and personal loss. They would also bring incredible sources of joy: finding jobs I loved, getting married, and having children. Thankfully, I made it through my twenties fully set up to thrive in my thirties. I managed to figure things out along the way.

I wish that ten years ago I had known what I needed to. I wish I could have had all that knowledge in one place. I wish I could have had this book.

I realized I wasn't alone. My friends and peers were struggling as well. Many newly minted adults are more educated than ever, yet more lost than ever. They face questions such as: How do I budget my money? How do I ace my first job? How should my relationships with my parents develop as I get older? How am I supposed to find my soul mate?

In general, none of these topics are covered in K–12 or college courses. We are expected to magically know them.

In the education world, one common objection goes, "You can't teach these things. They must be learned through experience." I disagree. We don't hand car keys to a sixteen-year-old and say, "Go get into a couple accidents, that will teach you how to drive." We teach Driver's Ed preemptively. Similarly, we shouldn't expect adults to have a wreck of a relationship before learning how to love; or to get audited by the IRS before learning to pay their taxes; or to die with regret before learning how to lead a fulfilling life.

So, I created and taught the course Adulting 101 at Boston College. I felt like I was uniquely qualified to put multiple crucial topics together. I had worked at startups in mental health and personal finance, started a successful nonprofit related to communication skills, and built a career that began in management consulting and led me to eventually run an off-the-record community for some of the most interesting leaders in the world.

The course became incredibly popular: Each time, it filled up within moments of registration opening and was the top-rated course in the department. And, through post-graduation surveys, I collected evidence that the curriculum was actually useful in the real world and influenced people's lives significantly. Over time, I turned the fourteen-week curriculum into a fourteen-chapter book.[1]

In other words, I've dedicated my adult life to gathering this knowledge and figuring out how to teach it to others in as simple and concise a way as possible. I've figured out the essence of adulting... so that you don't have to figure it out for yourself.

However, all this knowledge is pointless

—unless you know what you want. What's the point of knowing how to invest money if you don't know what you're saving for? What's the point of knowing how to date if you don't know what kind of relationship you want? What's the point of trying to become happy if you don't know what will make you happy?

Quick definitional note, to get it out of the way: I don't think "happiness" is quite the right word. I think everyone is trying to optimize for a good, meaningful life—for fulfillment over the long term. Let's call it long-term fulfillment, or "LTF" for short.

[1] In choosing which topics to include in the book, I asked myself, "Is this easily Google-able or ChatGPT-able?" For example, you can always Google how long something lasts in the fridge, but if you try to Google "should I get life insurance?" you will have a very hard time getting a straight answer—and probably not one that teaches the underlying principles in a step-by-step way. There are certainly other books that cover each of the topics in this one, but I think most young people are too busy to read fourteen different books—especially ones that go into way too much depth—rather than start with all of the basics, in one place, before embarking on their journey into adulthood.

How do you obtain LTF? In other words: What is the purpose of life?

Stop! I hate that question! Implicit in the question are not just one, but *three* myths about purpose.

1. **"*the* purpose"** – There is no one universal purpose. Everyone has their own variations.
2. **"purpose" (singular)** – You don't only have one purpose. You probably have many. Life is rarely about the mindless pursuit of one thing; it's often about diversifying your assets of meaning (more on this in skill #6).
3. **"of life" (implying a fixed point in time)** – Your purposes almost certainly won't stay the same. They will evolve as you learn and grow.

So, the more appropriate framing of the question is: "What are your *purposes* of life right now?"

Enter: the Google Doc

To answer that question, let's imagine a Google Doc listing all of your deepest wants.

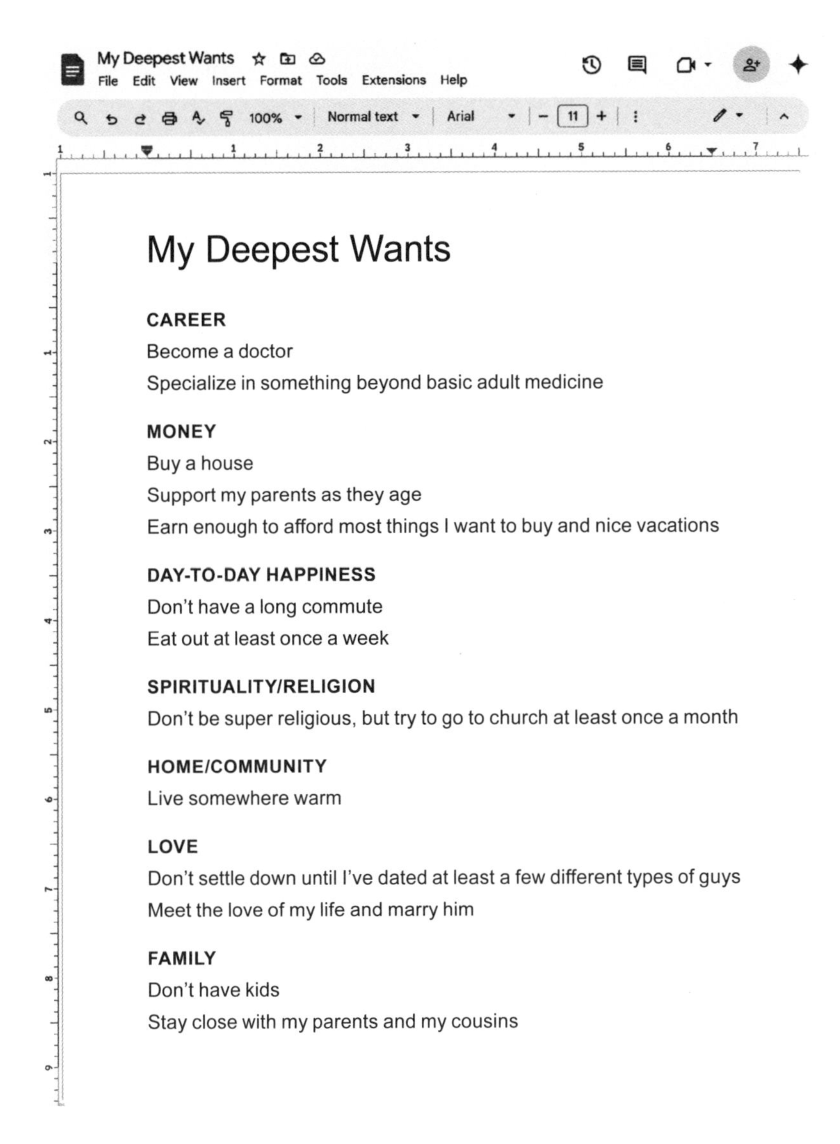
My Deepest Wants

CAREER
Become a doctor
Specialize in something beyond basic adult medicine

MONEY
Buy a house
Support my parents as they age
Earn enough to afford most things I want to buy and nice vacations

DAY-TO-DAY HAPPINESS
Don't have a long commute
Eat out at least once a week

SPIRITUALITY/RELIGION
Don't be super religious, but try to go to church at least once a month

HOME/COMMUNITY
Live somewhere warm

LOVE
Don't settle down until I've dated at least a few different types of guys
Meet the love of my life and marry him

FAMILY
Don't have kids
Stay close with my parents and my cousins

You'll create this doc yourself for homework (stay tuned). As you do, you'll probably start to wonder: "Where did these beliefs about what I want come from?" Let's open the doc's revision history.

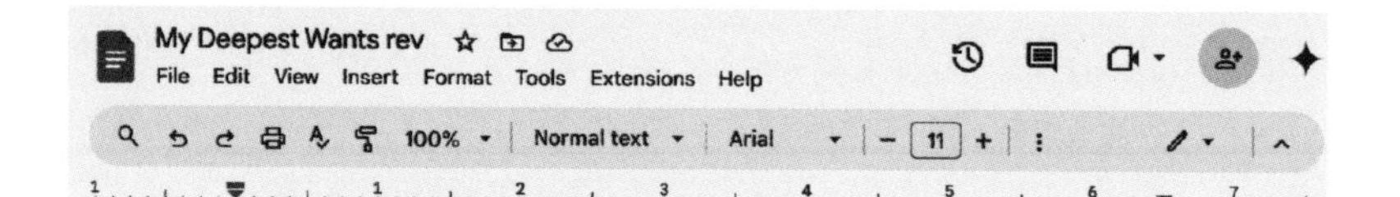

My Deepest Wants rev

CAREER

Become a doctor **Grandparents** - *they were poor and always told me I had a talent for it*

Specialize in something beyond basic adult medicine **Julia's dad** - *he's a doctor and told me he always wishes he had specialized (I think he just said this to me one time?)*

MONEY

Buy a house **Parents** - *they always said that buying a house is the most important step of adult life*

Support my parents as they age **Myself** - *I saw how they took care of my grandparents and I want to pay it forward*

Earn enough to afford most things I want to buy and nice vacations **Parents/me** - *we could never afford nice vacations and I was jealous of my friends who could*

DAY-TO-DAY HAPPINESS

Don't have a long commute **Myself** - *I hate hate hate driving in traffic*

Eat out at least once a week **College friends** - *they always go out and seem to look forward to it*

SPIRITUALITY/RELIGION

Don't be super religious, but still try to go to church at least once a month **Parents** - *that's what they did and it seemed to work*

HOME/COMMUNITY

Live somewhere warm **Myself** - *I can't stand the cold*

LOVE

Don't settle down until I've dated at least a few very different types of guys **Me? What I've heard from others?** - *it seems like everything I've watched shows how marriages can go wrong if you didn't experiment enough beforehand*

Meet the love of my life and marry him **Myself** - *I really want to be deeply loved, and to give a part of my life to someone else*

FAMILY

Don't have kids **Myself?** - *I've been babysitting a lot and realized I don't love being around kids. You need to really love it, right?*

Stay close with my parents and my cousins **Grandparents** - *they always told me family are the only people who will always look out for you no matter what*

As you can see, some of these beliefs may be hard-won—tested through experience, questioned, and re-questioned. But most were instilled by others. Until now, those beliefs have never been tested (let alone revealed that you have them!). Those are . . .

Hollow beliefs

Here's how to tell if a belief about what you want is hollow: If you thought about it deeply now, would you still believe it?

In some cases, the answer will be yes—the belief may have come from your parents, but you still truly do believe it, for your own reasons—and it can now graduate from hollow belief to hard-won belief. In other cases, the answer will be no—and you must discard the hollow belief to build a new belief from the ground up, based on your own ideas and experiences.

Many hollow beliefs come from randomly specific people at randomly specific times in life. For example, you may be attracted to people with a specific body type because that's the type of person the most popular kid in your high school class was dating—and you made the unconscious inference that if the most popular person wants to be with someone who has this body type, it must be the best (more myths about dating and attraction to come in skill #10). A surprising number of hollow beliefs come from movies, TV shows, books, and songs, whose words seemingly passed through us at the time, but whose messages wormed their way into our minds (more on this in skill #3).

You must go through every belief, one at a time, and question if you still believe it. You must question everything.

If this sounds suspiciously like having a quarter-life crisis . . . good! I think most people end up having midlife crises because it takes them a long time to realize they are living a life that they never chose. They wake up one day asking, "Do I really want to be married to this person? Do I really want to be in this career?" Their perceived lack of agency leads to a feeling of emptiness, which they desperately try to fill with things that feel novel: affairs or expensive cars or running away from home to travel the world, as the clichés go.

Of course, you may change as you get older. Revising your beliefs as you grow is good—but never having built hard-won beliefs to follow in the first place is not. I *want* you to have a quarter-life crisis now so that you won't have a midlife crisis later.

I had a quarter-life crisis related to one of my purposes about two years into my first job out of college. I realized that I had picked my job at Bain & Company, a prestigious management consulting company, solely because it was prestigious. During my senior year of college, I didn't know what I wanted to do, so I followed the heuristic that had served me well in my life until then: Aim for the thing that is hardest to get. Get the best grades, get into the best college, get the best job. But when it comes to jobs, there is no "best"—there's only the one that is best suited to you and your unique superpowers (more on that in skill #13).

I realized that all my life choices up to that point had been following one path. But it wasn't a path I dreamed up. The "achievement mindset" that pushed me to aim for the most prestigious choices was subconsciously instilled by my parents (immigrants to the United States who motivated me to work hard in school), teachers (who believed in me and had high hopes for me—"you have so much potential"), and my peers (especially in the hypercompetitive environment of Princeton). Many of these people meant well, but this combination of inputs created one big hollow belief.

In other words, I realized that I was living life according to what I thought others expected me to do.

The science of adult development

Modern psychology has validated these insights with research. This field is called "adult development." The theory posits that just as children go through developmental stages, so do adults. But whereas the stages of children are necessarily tied to their age (for example, it's impossible for a one-year-old child to form entire sentences, but when they hit the two- or three-year mark, they can), the stages of adults are not necessarily tied to age.

That's bad news and good news. The bad: You can get stuck in perpetual adolescence (as with some people I'm sure you know). The good: You can evolve to higher stages more rapidly. It's all up to you.

Different adult development scientists define these stages differently, but the most general formulation is as follows.

Stage 1. The Impulsive Mind – blindly following your impulses (often tied to childhood)

Stage 2. The Imperial Mind – following your desires in the moment, with little regard for the future or the needs of others (often tied to adolescence)

Stage 3. The Socialized Mind – mostly caring about what you think others expect from you

Stage 4. The Self-Authored Mind – mostly caring about what you want to do

Stage 5. The Self-Transforming Mind – being able to hold multiple seemingly contradictory beliefs in equal regard

What we've been discussing so far is the transition from Stage 3 to Stage 4, from the socialized mind to the self-authored mind. The vast majority of adults are stuck (for their entire lives!) in the socialized mind. This book—and the work you do while reading it—will help you evolve to the self-authored mind.[2]

Getting to the self-authored mind requires naming what you think you want, identifying where that belief came from, questioning whether it's right, and forming new beliefs—along a range of dimensions. We'll get there.

For the time being, think of it this way: Your whole life, you've had read-only access to the Google Doc of your deepest wants; now, for the first time, you've been granted edit access.

How to get the most out of this book

For each topic, we will aim to address not only "*how* do I get what I want?" (the knowledge you need) but also to help you first answer the question "*what* do I want?"

Reading this book will be an active experience, not a passive one. You'll be asked to stop reading and to reflect, to take notes, and to write down answers to questions. None of this information will serve you if you don't integrate it into your own life.[3]

I have three important requests:

1. Please read one chapter at a time – This book is intended to be snackable, not bingeable. Each topic is a bite-size snack, to be consumed (and interacted with) one at a time.

2 For any overachievers here: Apparently only 1% of adults ever reach Stage 5.

3 A brief disclaimer, before we go any further: Nothing in this book constitutes official financial advice, tax advice, or legal advice. When sharing information on these topics, I have tried to include all relevant facts, peppered with my own opinions. My aim is to share the knowledge you need to make the best possible decisions. But before making an important financial decision, consult a finance professional; for a tax decision, consult a tax professional; for legal advice, consult a lawyer (and your conscience). In other words, please don't sue me. K, thanks.

2. Please keep a notebook handy – I'll give you some thought exercises and practice questions. Keep an eye out for the pencil icon throughout to indicate when it's time to put these skills into practice.

3. Please do the homework – Each chapter ends with an assignment to do in your life. Don't move on to the next chapter until you've completed the assignment and reflected on that experience.

Of course, you don't *have* to do any of this. Weren't you listening? Don't live your life according to my expectations for you!

SUMMARY

- Most people's education never taught them what they need to know for adult life; this book has that knowledge in one place.
- That knowledge is only useful if you know what you actually want; the proper question is, "What are the purposes of your life right now?"
- The Google Doc of your deepest wants was mostly authored by others (hollow beliefs); in order to transition from the socialized mind to the self-authored mind, you must begin revising it.

Homework

You guessed it! Write and revise the Google Doc of your deepest wants.

1. Write down one or two beliefs for each category in the template from above. (Many of the categories listed are universal, but yours are likely somewhat different, so feel free to adapt them.)
2. For each belief, label who it comes from.
3. Then label whether it's a hard-won belief or a hollow belief.
4. For each hollow belief, cross it out and start writing a new (draft! tentative! work-in-progress!) belief.

Extra credit: Share your updated Google Doc with a close friend. Ask them, "Do you think I am being honest with myself about what I wrote?"

I.

Mental Skills

Skill #2

FACE REJECTION

During my sophomore year of college, I developed a crush on a freshman girl. We spent nearly one week hanging out together. I asked her out on a date, and, in a very gentle and roundabout way, she rejected me.

I was involved in a political advocacy student group. When election time came, I ran for president. I was outvoted. They gave me the option to drop down to the election for vice president, which I took. I lost again. Then I dropped down to treasurer. And lost.

I was very involved in theater on campus, having acted in numerous plays during my freshman year. I applied to direct a play the following year and was rejected. I auditioned for two other plays and didn't make the cast list.

I was very keen on becoming a residential advisor, thinking I had a lot to offer new students to help them adjust to college life. So I applied for that job—and was rejected. I was also looking for a summer internship and became interested in management consulting. I applied, and was invited to interview. I felt that this was going to be my thing—they gave me a lot of positive encouragement, and

I thought I would be great at it. I remember wanting that internship so badly that I could feel a burning sensation in my stomach when I thought about it. After the interview, I got rejected.

Finally, before the February break, I "bickered" (rushed) for an eating club, Princeton's version of Greek life (except instead of living together, you eat together). The process mostly involved games and icebreakers. I felt like I really fit in, I was making a good impression, I was on fire—then I got rejected.

My college career was halfway over, and it felt like everything I had been building had fallen out from under me. I felt talentless and unlikable.

On a whim, I decided to get away from campus for the February break and visit a friend in Arizona. While hiking on a gorgeous mountain in the crisp desert air, I reflected on my winter of rejection. Why did it hurt so badly?

What we tell ourselves about rejection

Before I tell you my answer, I want you to come up with your answer and write it in your notebook.

What are two things you attempted recently that you really wanted, but were rejected for?

Upon reflection, what was it about these rejections that hurt?

I identified three reasons the rejections during my sophomore year had particularly hurt:

1. I felt like I was being rejected as a person – The more I thought that a particular opportunity was the right fit for me, the more painful the rejection was. It was as if someone (an employer, a potential date) had asked, "Are you this type of person?" and I said, "Yes, yes! That's me!" and then they said, "No, it's not." My identity had overlapped with the opportunity in exciting ways, and then my identity was called into question.

2. I wanted to be seen as someone naturally successful – I was always good at school, and I liked cultivating the image of someone who was naturally smart, who could get an A without studying very much. I wanted to be seen as the kind of person to whom things come easily. Adversity was fine, but only to the extent that it benefited my narrative; in my obituary they'd write, "This one time he was rejected, but then he got something even better, and boy did he show them!" The series of rejections was ruining that narrative.

3. The rejections were the end of everything good in my life – Until then, my life overall had been on an upward trajectory. Now, it felt like so many things I cared about were taken away from me. If I couldn't even get a role in a play, that was the end of my theater career. If I couldn't get that summer internship, when I thought my chances were so good, I wouldn't be able to get another one. If I couldn't get a date with a girl who I thought liked me, I would never get another date.

As you can probably tell, none of these were quite true. They were gross exaggerations of a small grain of truth—lies I was telling myself that discouraged me from wanting to keep trying.

What I didn't see at the time was that these rejections hadn't made me weaker, *they had made me stronger*. I now had real-life evidence that being thoroughly rejected didn't end the world.

Over time, I learned truths to counteract each of the above lies:

1. Rejections don't imply anything significant about you as a person – As a thought experiment, imagine there's an opportunity that you are truly the right fit for (if they accept you, you will excel). Now imagine they reject you. If, objectively, you would have been their best pick, then it cannot be that they rejected you because they took a holistic look at you and determined you're not good enough. It must be because they didn't look at you *enough*.

We often fear the judgment of people who know us least. Which is really silly, when you think about it—if they don't know you well, they are likely missing the inside view of all your positive qualities. (For that reason, the people whose criticism I most listen to are the ones who know me best.)

For example, when I was on the other side of the job-application process, I was shocked by how little time we took to review resumes. I was sent a file with over 150 resumes and had less than two hours to evaluate them all. If you do the math, that's one resume per forty-eight seconds. Forty-eight seconds! How can you judge someone in that amount of time? You can't. In the end, most of my decisions were probably based on random phrases that stood out while skimming the resume, or even my mood at the time. Behavioral economists have studied how something as simple as the time of day can determine a judge's willingness to grant a parole request.

It's shocking how many rejections are caused by chance. For example, my wife, Charlotte, reworked her senior thesis (about maternal care in French Guiana) into a book in French. She submitted the manuscript to three different academic publishers in France. Two of them rejected her, and the third never responded. She began to question the whole endeavor: "Why did I think anyone would want to read this in the first place? I was being ridiculous for trying to get this published. I am a bad writer." Over one year later, she was surprised to receive a letter from that publisher. They had lost the original query and later found it; they apologized for the delay, and offered to publish her book!

2. Everyone encounters rejection (no matter how successful they seem) – Charlotte's great-aunt is incredibly successful; she won the MacArthur "genius" grant for founding a freestanding birth center to help underserved women. When we went to visit her, the hallways of her apartment were covered with framed awards and certificates. When she showed us into the guest room, we noticed about a dozen colored sashes hanging from a coat rack. "What are those?" I asked. "Oh, those are my honorary doctorates."

But then she told us about her life, about the many years of work before the awards came in. About her grant applications that had been rejected. About the prominent people who had called her inept, who publicly criticized her. She worked each day to convince the medical establishment that she wasn't crazy, that the birth centers she was supporting were even safer than hospitals for low-risk pregnancies, and that poor women deserved access to quality care. The awards and sashes only came at the end of the story, a sort of coda.

No one is "naturally" successful. Everyone who receives a lot of recognition spent a great deal of time *not* receiving a lot of recognition.[4]

3. Rejections can be for the best – Not only did my winter of rejection not end everything good in my life, but it actually led to good. Scaling back my involvement in politics and theater helped me focus on other things I enjoyed a lot more.

That internship I applied to? I applied again the next year. This time, I was . . . rejected! But then I applied again the following year, for a full-time job after college, and was accepted.

That girl I asked out? We still spent a lot of time together. After many months, I felt like I was finally getting over her. But then, my heart would do somersaults every time we sat next to each other, and I gave up thinking we could be just friends. I asked her out again, and this time she said yes. (Turns out she had a long-distance boyfriend the first time I asked, but didn't want to tell me, because she didn't want me to stop liking her.) If I had never asked her out in the first place, we wouldn't have dated, and become engaged, and I

4 A couple of my favorite examples from the literary world: Khaled Hosseini, who wrote *The Kite Runner*, was rejected by more than thirty literary agents. Frank Herbert, who wrote the seminal sci-fi novel *Dune*, was rejected by more than twenty publishers (before he was finally published—by a company that printed auto repair manuals).

wouldn't now be married to the most amazing woman in the world (for me—see skill #10).

Of course, not every rejection ends up being for the best. Sometimes you lose and you just have to try again. But would you rather end up having a track record of 100% success, or many accomplishments (along with many failures)? In other words, what most impacts your life is not your shots-on-goal-to-goals ratio, it's the number of goals.

Imagine you had no fear of rejection. That would be the ultimate superpower! You would be willing to try anything. You would put yourself in situations way "out of your league"—and sure, you might get rejected 99% of the time—but even winning 1% of the time would be enough to build an incredible life.

Weirdly, the only way to develop this superpower *is to get rejected*. A lot. Each time, the fear of getting rejected again diminishes a bit.

For that reason, the rejections you've received are not something to be ashamed of; they are something to be treasured. They are what got you to where you are, and what has built up your fledgling superpower of fearlessness.

Charlotte and I bought a little treasure chest. Every time we got rejected from a job opportunity, or a publication, or anything else, we printed the rejection letter, folded it, and placed it in the treasure chest. We didn't hide it; we displayed it proudly. It contained the sources of our strength.

Developing a growth mindset

The social scientist Carol Dweck identified two different mindsets people can have about aptitude. People with a "fixed" mindset believe that aptitude is unchanging, whereas people with a "growth" mindset believe aptitude can change. What's interesting is how many thoughts and behaviors stem from having a different core belief about this seemingly simple question.

Because people with a fixed mindset see aptitude as set in stone, they are more concerned with proving to others that they are smart than with getting smarter. When confronted with a mistake or with feedback, they are more inclined to double down on their choice or viewpoint. They can't admit they are wrong because that would mean admitting they are dumb! By contrast, people with a growth mindset take feedback eagerly because they know it is an opportunity to improve their aptitude. They don't want to waste time proving they are right or smart; they want to spend time getting better.

Whereas people with a fixed mindset avoid challenges—because they see them as a threat to their perceived intelligence—people with a growth mindset actively seek them out.

You can guess how people with a growth mindset face rejection . . . it's an opportunity to grow! People with a fixed mindset live in fear of rejection and thus are much less likely to put themselves out there.

There's no real way to "prove" whether aptitude is fixed or not; it's a belief (more to come about core beliefs in the next chapter). So, you can choose to have a growth mindset, and thus become more resilient, and—in the long term—much more likely to become successful.

How? Here are some basic techniques you can try:

1. Use the word "yet" when describing yourself or your accomplishments – Saying "I'm no good at tennis" is a fixed mindset type of thing to say. But saying "I'm no good at tennis *yet*" implies that you can change this—you can learn. Or, "I'm not qualified to apply for this job . . . yet" (implies you can get there one day).

2. Frame each new challenge as an experiment – If you're hesitant to try something new, call it an experiment. "I'm going to try writing a poem for the first time, and I'm interested to see what happens." In the best case, the experiment showed that you have potential (that you can keep growing); in the worst case, you learned that it isn't worth repeating.

The second tactic comes in especially handy when you're attempting something that you think will likely end in rejection. So what? It's an experiment! Just see what happens. Best case, you get what you wanted; worst case, you have a new addition to your treasure chest.

In our discussion of rejection so far, there's one question we have not (yet!) addressed: What happens when you *do* get the thing you want?

The contentment mindset

It may seem strange to frame an achievement as a negative. But for many people, getting what they want presents a major problem in their life—they now have to learn how to be happy with what they have.

Many of our desires (for a promotion, for a partner, for an accolade) are mirages: They give the illusion that if we obtain them, we will be happy. But once we get them, they vanish—because the moment of having gotten what you wanted lasts for . . . well, a moment.

Then it's over, and you ask yourself, "Now what?" And the natural follow-up question: "What do I need to go for next?" Many people are wired to constantly seek achievement—and actually *achieving* things doesn't satisfy that need. They always need more.

Thankfully, just as you can learn to transition from a fixed mindset to a growth mindset, you can transition from an "achievement" mindset to what I call a "contentment" mindset.

"Contentment" may sound like a state of being, but in fact it's a skill—it doesn't happen naturally. Getting what you want won't make you content; only looking at what you already have in a certain way will.

For example, let's say you bought stock in a company (which you'll learn how to do in skill #6), and the stock went down in value. You'd be unhappy, having lost money. Now assume the stock went up in value. You'd be happy then, right? Not necessarily! You could be thinking regretfully, "I wish I had bought even more of it. Then I would have made more money." (Conversely, even if you lose money, you can think happily, "I'm glad I didn't buy even more of that stock!")

Think of achievement as climbing a mountain. You believe that if you reach the summit, you will be content, but once you reach it you can now see another, even higher summit. With this metaphor in mind, here is how you can learn to feel like you have enough:

1. Don't forget to look down – When you reach a summit, peer below you and admire how far you've come. Taking the time to be grateful is incredibly powerful.

Another way of framing gratitude is to look forward to what you already have with the same vigor that you look forward to things you don't yet have. Remember what it was like to be at the bottom of the mountain—how you wished you could have what you have now! And now you do have it.

Whenever you need to look down, you can try the following exercise:

- Close your eyes.
- Think of something in your life that you deeply appreciate—a partner, a job, an accomplishment.
- Recall a time before you had that. Think about what it was like to be you, back then. Think about how much you wanted it. Try to feel that same sense of deep desire, in your mind and throughout your body.
- Now, open your eyes. Snap back to the present. You *have* that thing you wanted!

2. Set up camp for the night – No climber worth their salt (snow?) would keep climbing into the night. When you reach a summit, set up a warm fire and share a toast with your friends. In other words, celebrate! When you reach a milestone, you can tell your friends that you are happy and want to show your gratitude by taking them out to dinner. That way, your memories of achieving the thing will be tied to memories of sharing quality time with people you care about.

You have, *right now*, all the reasons you need to be unhappy, and you have all the reasons you need to be happy. Of course, there will always be goals worth aiming for—they might be able to make you even more content—but you won't *need* them in order to be content.

There's a story about when the philosopher Diogenes was asked by Alexander the Great's lieutenant, "Alexander has conquered half the world. What have you done?" Diogenes responded, "I have conquered the need to conquer the world."

SUMMARY

- Getting rejected may hurt in the moment, but it doesn't imply anything significant about you as a person, nor will it end everything good in your life; no one is "naturally" successful.
- Rejections are something to be treasured, because they make you stronger and help you attain the ultimate superpower (not being afraid to try anything).
- If you believe that your aptitude can change, you will benefit from mistakes and feedback; you can transition from a fixed mindset to a growth mindset by using the word "yet" and by framing new challenges as experiments.
- Contentment is a skill, not a state of being; you can transition from an achievement mindset to a contentment mindset by not forgetting to look down (appreciating how far you've come) and by setting up camp for the night (celebrating milestones with friends).

Homework

Intentionally try to get rejected from at least three things. For example, the next time you order coffee, ask if you can have it for free. No need to lie or beg, you can just say, "Any chance I could have this for free today? I would really appreciate it." But try to make at least one of these rejections something significant (for example, an aspirational job application).

Then, decorate a box to use as your rejection treasure chest. Every time you get rejected, print the message (or write a note about it) and put it in the box. Display it proudly in your home.

Extra credit: Write down three significant things that you previously really wanted or looked forward to that you now have. In your mind, try to look forward to having these things as you once did (before you had them).

Skill #3

THINK CRITICALLY

A friend in college was going through a tough time, and I was wondering what I could do to console him. That day, I walked through the library and saw this quote on a poster:

> *People will forget what you said, people will forget what you did, but people will never forget how you made them feel.*
> —Maya Angelou

I'd seen the quote before, and it seemed to finally hit home. My friend will forget what I do and what I say, but he won't forget how I make him feel. How do I make him feel better?

But wait . . . is this quote even true? I realized I wasn't sure. I've remembered plenty of things people said and did to me in life. And even if the quote were true, was it helpful? I can control what I say and what I do, but I cannot control how I make others feel. For example, I could compliment someone and that might backfire and make them feel angry if they thought I was being disingenuous. (In fact, how people feel is often an inaccurate reflection of reality—we'll cover this in much more detail in the next chapter.)

Yes, Maya Angelou was a famous writer; she was nominated for a Pulitzer Prize and a Tony Award; she won multiple Grammy Awards; and her face was plastered on posters with beautiful quotes across libraries the world over. But in this case, in my humble opinion, she was wrong.

Which made me wonder . . . who else is wrong? What other untrue ideas have I been unconsciously following?

Sturgeon's law

I have since become a fan of "Sturgeon's law," popularized by the philosopher Daniel Dennett: 90% of everything you hear or read is total bullshit.

People say a lot of things. People write a lot of things. Many of them are, at best, misleading or incomplete; at worst, totally false. I don't think most people are intentional liars. But humans are prone to all kinds of biases and assumptions that distort what they say.

This even applies to most of what you learned in college. For example, years after I took Introduction to Macroeconomics I discovered that almost every topic in the course was taught through the lens of Keynesian theory; a theory that is popular and well respected, but also one theory among many that economists fiercely debate. I had gone into the world thinking I knew the basics of macroeconomics, while in fact I had such a narrow view of the topic that it was utterly useless, even counterproductive—in other words, BS.

To me, critical thinking means questioning the validity of everything you see and hear, in order to better develop your own worldview. According to a study conducted by the career coaching organization 80,000 Hours, critical thinking is the second most employable skill—with the lowest risk of being replaced by AI—across all fields (second only to "good judgment"). It's more useful in any job you take than time management, spoken communication, or any hard skill like writing or programming.

The CAR process

Of course . . . that study may be BS, too. So might this entire chapter—and this entire book! I try to write as accurately as possible, but, of course, I have my own biases and blind spots. Only you can determine what is true.

To do so, here is a process for critical thinking that I dubbed **CAR: Comprehend**, **Analyze**, **Revise**.

1. Comprehend: What are they saying?

Before you worry about whether something you read is true, you must first understand what the statement is really trying to convey. Sometimes this is easy; for example, if you read a straightforward claim like "Six people in the United States died this year from tripping on a garden hose." Other times it can be difficult; for example, if you read "Garden hoses are incredibly dangerous"—what exactly does "dangerous" mean? Compared to what? You may have to dive into the fine print to understand what the claim is.

This gets trickier with messages that are conveyed by stories in TV shows, song lyrics, and, of course, poetry (sorry, Maya). Even stories that are entirely fictional often *imply* things about the way people are or the way the world is. It takes some reflection to figure out what an artist is trying to convey—or, more importantly (since often their intentions are unknowable), what you think the story has conveyed.

2. Analyze: Do I agree?

To answer that question, utilize your common sense, life experiences, and the entire corpus of knowledge in your head. But one counterargument isn't enough—go through multiple iterations of "on the one hand, on the other hand" to tease out the deeper layers.

For example, let's evaluate the claim "Everyone should have the right to free speech." We often take this one for granted (and I happen to believe it), but the reasons are not so simple.

On the one hand, what if someone uses their right to free speech to intentionally offend someone else? On the other hand, who gets to deem what is offensive? Someone could claim that being told garden hoses are totally safe offends them and ban others from saying it.

On the other hand, it doesn't seem crazy to have some universal standards for what kind of speech is beyond the pale. For example, the law doesn't let anyone use their right to free speech to incite violence. So, clearly, the right shouldn't protect *all* speech. On the other hand, if we start banning certain kinds of speech, we won't be banning that *thought*—people may still think vile things, and now we won't have an accurate understanding of what the populace believes.

On the other *other* hand . . . You get the point. I could do this all day! But at some point, you'll arrive at a conclusion—and most of the time, the claim you are evaluating won't be a timeless philosophical quandary, so the process will be much quicker. (For example, "No, I don't think garden hoses are that dangerous.")

3. Revise: What do I now believe?

A. If you agree with the claim, you now need to incorporate it into your worldview. Which existing beliefs does it challenge, or force you to adapt?

B. If you disagree with the claim, build an argument against it—one that can convince others (just as you've been convinced) that it's false. And, think of the negative consequences of other people believing the claim.

C. If you're unsure, what more evidence would you need in order to believe or disbelieve the claim? And, where can you start looking for that evidence?

Let's do an example. Song lyrics are powerful, and we are constantly (unconsciously!) learning messages from them. As of the time of this writing, "Flowers" by Miley Cyrus is the top song of the year. In the chorus, she sings about being afraid to leave her boyfriend and then realizing that she can buy herself flowers, to love herself "better than you can."

1. Comprehend – Miley seemed afraid to break up with her boyfriend because she didn't want to be alone, but now she realizes that all of the needs that he satisfied (buying her flowers, talking with her) she can do by herself just as well. In other words, she can be just as happy without him.

2. Analyze – Can single people be just as happy as people in long-term relationships? On the one hand, plenty of research shows that people in committed relationships on average are happier than those who are not. On the other hand, it depends on the relationship—if someone is with a partner who is very wrong for them, they would be much happier on their own. On the other hand, that doesn't mean they need to be committed to remaining single; having your hand held (the warmth and intimacy of human touch) is a need you can never satisfy for yourself.

3. Revise – I do not agree with the claim. So how would I convince someone else? "I still believe that, although people in bad relationships should usually end them, there are certain human needs that only other people can fulfill. Just as Miley is right to not be afraid to break up, she should also not be afraid to try again and keep searching for a life partner who can make her happy."

Furthermore, I do think that people who become unconsciously influenced by this song may be harmed by it. They risk becoming complacent about the search for a life partner—and justifying that complacency by citing Miley's (alleged!)[5] happiness.

As you can see, your conclusion may not always be a "yes" or "no" answer. Often, through this process, you'll uncover nuance in the message and arrive at your own layered answer.

That's a lot of thinking to do for just one song! The words we listen to on the radio or Spotify may seem irrelevant at the time, but they have a way of worming their way into our minds and, eventually, our entire worldviews. Critical thinking is also why I tend

5 At the time of this writing, she has a boyfriend again.

to read so slowly. Nearly every sentence makes some claim about people or the world, and I feel the need to dissect it.[6]

Perhaps I go overboard. Of course, it's not always worth it; sometimes you just want to enjoy the music, or turn your brain off. That's fine.

But, be careful about not doing this enough. In the internet era, information comes at us faster than we can process it. Seemingly everyone with an opinion tweets it or makes a TikTok video about it—as a result, it seems like the average person probably spends 80% of their time consuming content and only 20% thinking about it. I think the more ideal balance is closer to 20% consuming and 80% thinking. Otherwise, we risk letting these opinions infiltrate our worldviews unquestioned.

Think of your mind as a Brita water filter. Water (new information and opinions) gets poured in through the top. Your filter (mind) seeks to comprehend, analyze, and revise your existing beliefs in response to it. The water that passes through the filter makes it down into the jug (your worldview). It's clean and delicious.

However, if you pour too much water at the top, the filter cannot process it fast enough, and the water spills over the top. Now you've ended up with dirty, unfiltered water mixed in your jug.

6 It becomes easier the more you do it; questioning new viewpoints can become just as unconscious as absorbing them. Partly because so much of what you hear is the same stuff repeated over and over in different words (that's what makes new ideas so exciting!).

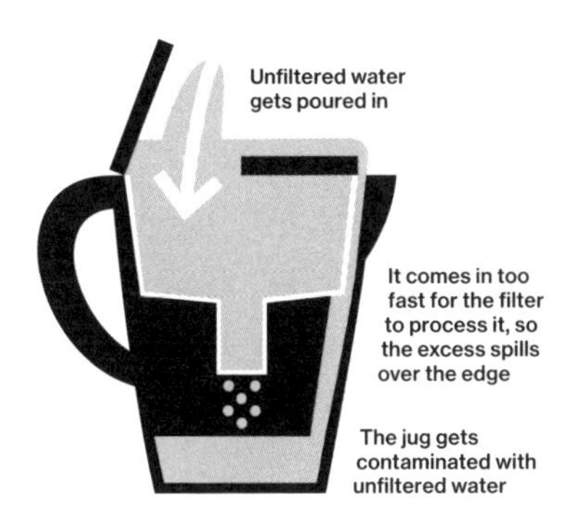

In other words, you've ended up with all kinds of opinions whose validity you've never tested. You might find yourself saying "I believe X," but when someone asks you why, you're stumped. In other words: They are hollow beliefs. Critical thinking—and consuming content slowly enough to let your filter work its CAR magic—is the only way to end up with fewer hollow beliefs. Being a grown-up means taking responsibility for what you believe to be true.

SUMMARY

- **90% of everything you read or hear is bullshit (Sturgeon's law); that's why you must think critically (question the validity of everything you read or hear).**
- **To do so, you can use the CAR process: Comprehend ("What are they saying?"), Analyze ("Do I agree?"), and Revise ("What existing beliefs do I now need to change?").**
- **Try to transition from spending 80% of your time consuming and 20% thinking to the opposite; otherwise, your Brita filter will overflow and you'll end up with unfiltered water in your jug (which become hollow beliefs).**

Homework

The next time you read an article or a chapter in a book, stop at the first sentence that you think is making a claim about people or the world. Go through the full CAR process in writing.

Extra credit: The next time a song comes on, try to parse what the song is trying to say. Go through the full CAR process in your head.

Skill #4

REFRAME AUTOMATIC THOUGHTS

It's Saturday night and you're feeling down.

You and your friend had agreed you'd be in touch tonight about plans. You texted her, but she didn't respond. You waited and waited . . . nothing. You thought, "She's probably mad at me." Then you racked your brain for all the things you may have done or said to upset her. You are angry at yourself, frustrated with her, and sad about the looming plans-free night.

The next morning, you get a text:

> *soooo sorry about last night! My brother had an emergency and I had to take him to the ER, my phone died*

It turns out, your feelings last night were based on a thought that turned out to be not true ("She's probably mad at me"). As I'm sure you've experienced, this kind of thing happens all the time.

That's because your feelings are not always right. Often, you should *not* listen to your heart.

The feelings equation

The Stoic philosopher Epictetus wrote:

> What really frightens and dismays us is not external events themselves, but the way in which we think about them. It is not things that disturb us, but our interpretation of their significance.

In other words: It's not what happens, but rather your thoughts about what happens that impacts how you feel.

For example: You're on the top floor of a tall office building. The fire alarm goes off. "Oh no, there's a fire!" you think. You scramble to get to the staircase. "How am I going to make it down all these flights of stairs?" you think as you plead with your legs to move faster. You are anxious, panicked, and sweating.

Alternatively: You're on the top floor of a tall office building. The fire alarm goes off. "Here we go again, another drill," you think. You calmly pack your things into your bag and grab a cup of water from the cooler on your way to the stairs. You are relaxed, slightly annoyed, and hydrated.

Of course, there is an objective truth—either the building is on fire or it isn't!—and that matters. But the example goes to show how, in the moment, it's only the reaction in your head that matters to how you *feel*.

Let's say your friend is hosting a potluck and you put a lot of time into baking a rich chocolate cake. At the party, you see someone taking a bite and commenting out loud, "Whoa."

Are you thinking, "Whoa, this cake blew them away—I am a master baker!"

Or are you thinking, "Whoa, they couldn't believe how bad this cake is—I am a failure!"

Again, it may seem dramatic to label yourself either a "master baker" or a "failure" based on your attempted interpretation of the tone in someone's one word. But we do this all the time. And then, based on that label, we may go on to act differently in the moment (brag to everyone that the cake is yours, versus leave the party early) or even in the long term (enroll in a cooking class, versus never try to bake again).

We can summarize this in an equation:

Behavior = Input + Thoughts + Feelings

In other words, there is an input (something happens), and depending on how you think about it, you'll feel a certain way, then depending on how you feel, you'll act a certain way.

The problem is, as we saw in these examples, your thoughts are often inaccurate.

In the 1960s, psychiatrists like Aaron Beck transformed these ancient insights into a technique that has since been validated as one of the most effective, evidence-based forms of psychotherapy: cognitive behavioral therapy (CBT). One of the main ideas of CBT is that, sometimes, our automatic thoughts aren't accurate. However, we can take a step back and evaluate whether they're true.

CBT identifies about a dozen different categories that these "thought errors" can fall under. We'll focus on four of them:

1. Jumping to conclusions
2. All-or-nothing thinking
3. Labeling
4. Emotional reasoning

1. Jumping to conclusions – That means skipping ahead to a particular conclusion, without enough evidence.

Let's say you give a big presentation at work. At the end of the meeting, as everyone is heading out, your boss gives you a quick "good job." You think, "I can tell he's only saying that sarcastically. I bet he actually thinks I'm not adding value. No one ever takes my ideas seriously."

What is the potentially false conclusion in there? In fact, there are at least three!

> *I can tell he's only saying that sarcastically.* How can you tell? Maybe because he had a certain tone of voice? But then again, maybe that's just how he talks. Maybe because he walked out after saying that to you? But then again, maybe he was rushing to another meeting. There's no way of really knowing what he was thinking. That's because you're not a mind reader!
>
> *I bet he actually thinks I'm not adding value.* Even if what you shared was stupid (despite the compliment), you have no evidence that he thinks you're not adding any value at work.
>
> *No one ever takes my ideas seriously.* That can't possibly be true. Maybe in this case someone didn't take your ideas seriously, but it certainly hasn't happened with every idea you've ever had.

2. All-or-nothing thinking – This is the tendency to see things in black or white categories. It often involves words like "everything," "always," or "never."

For example, "This always happens to me." That thought is actually pretty funny, when you think about it. How can any one thing *always* happen to you? Surely there are other things that happen to you as well!

The thought about your boss is also an example of all-or-nothing thinking: "No one ever takes my ideas seriously." That's unlikely! (And yes, some thoughts can be exemplary of multiple thought errors.)

These dichotomous thoughts are precisely the opposite of how the world works. Good things don't *never* happen to you. There is not one problem that's causing *all* the misfortune in the world. The truth is often a balance between the "always" and the "never," between the "all" and the "nothing."

I've personally tried to eliminate those words from my vocabulary because they are (almost) never accurate.

3. Labeling – Labeling is describing the whole of something by one of its traits.

For example, you can label yourself: "I'm a slow learner" or "I'm such a loser." But this is total nonsense! You aren't any one thing. The psychiatrist David Burns, who helped popularize CBT, wrote: "Would you think of yourself exclusively as an 'eater' just because you eat, or a 'breather' just because you breathe?"

Some other examples:

> *I don't feel like finishing this right now. I'm so lazy.* Just because you aren't in the mood for work doesn't mean you're a lazy person.
>
> *If I don't go to the party tonight, then I'm antisocial.* Just because you skip one party doesn't mean you're an antisocial person.
>
> *Sometimes I talk to myself; I must be crazy.* Just because you talk to yourself sometimes doesn't mean you're an insane person.

It's possible to label not only yourself, but also others: "She's an idiot" or "He's a bad person." That colors your perception of them and often becomes a self-fulfilling prophecy. Once you see someone as stupid, you'll likely engage in confirmation bias to overemphasize their mistakes and discount the intelligent things they do say.

4. Emotional reasoning – Emotional reasoning means assuming that if you feel a certain way, then it must be true.

For example: "I feel sad, therefore something must have happened to make me sad." As we just learned, that's not always true. If you feel sad, it could be that something bad happened, but it could also be that something neutral (or even good) happened, and you had unrealistically negative thoughts about it.

Another example: "I feel guilty, therefore I must have done something bad."

You may feel guilty because you think you accidentally said something hurtful. But maybe what you said wasn't that bad at all. So you have no reason to feel guilty.

Even if we're aware of emotional reasoning, it can be difficult to avoid in real life. Our emotions feel so real—and they are real! But they're based on our thoughts, which may or may not be correct.

Practice time

Let's take an example similar to our first one:

> My friend hasn't texted me back, and it's been two days. He must be mad at me. It makes sense, since he's easily offended.

Which types of thought errors are present here? Take a moment to review and think about it before looking at the answer.

Answer: jumping to conclusions and labeling.

"He must be mad at me" is a conclusion for which there isn't sufficient evidence. He might be mad at you, but he might also be really busy. Or, he turned off his phone for the weekend while out on a trip. Or, he left his phone on top of his car, then drove away (like my wife has done—more than once). Unless you ask him, you can't know how he feels. Remember, you're not a mind reader.

In addition, "He's easily offended" is an example of labeling others. Perhaps there are times when he's taken offense, but surely you've also said things at some point that didn't offend him. Seeing him in this light will make you think about the times he acted in a touchy way, while ignoring examples of his resilience.

For that same reason, labeling yourself makes it harder to change and grow. If you assume "I'm a bad presenter," you'll automatically emphasize examples of that being true while ignoring times when it's not true.

How about this one?

> I always feel lonely at night. I don't have enough friends.

That thought has both all-or-nothing thinking and emotional reasoning. (If you got it wrong: You are a slow learner and you will never understand this. Just kidding!)

"I always feel lonely at night" is all-or-nothing. There are definitely some nights when you're with other people, or you're by yourself but don't feel lonely. (Words like "all" or "never" are good hints of all-or-nothing thinking.)

The other one is a bit more subtle. Thinking "I don't have enough friends" just because you feel lonely doesn't seem accurate. Especially because "enough friends" is so arbitrary! What is enough? Three friends? Thirty? Three hundred? Even having one friend is enough to alleviate loneliness.

You may feel lonely for other reasons: You haven't talked to your long-distance friends in a while, or you miss your family, or, most likely, *you just feel lonely*. Sometimes we feel lonely or disconnected for no particular reason. Just because you feel that way doesn't mean there's something inherently wrong with your social life or your love life.

One last example:

> I didn't do a good job with the memo for work. I missed some glaring mistakes! I should prepare more if I want to do better next time.

Which thought errors are present here?

None (trick question, sorry). Not doing "a good job" isn't a logical leap of any kind. A thought error might have been "I never do a good job" (all-or-nothing thinking). And, wanting to prepare more in order "to do better next time" sounds like a pretty reasonable plan.

A thought error would have been "no matter how much I prepare, I'll still do poorly" (jumping to conclusions).

Life-changing results

I don't know about you, but the first time I learned about thought errors, it was mind-blowing. On the one hand, it's so obvious (of course the thoughts in those examples aren't true)—but then again, no one ever taught me to notice untrue thoughts.

That's the first step of CBT: noticing your thought errors. Then, if you can identify which type of thought error it is, you can reframe it into a more accurate thought (we'll practice that shortly).

And as we learned, a more accurate thought will lead to a different emotion, which will lead to a different behavior. It sounds so simple, but it actually alters your brain chemistry. Building this basic habit has lifted many people out of depression and anxiety. Studies were done in which people's brains were scanned after a course in CBT and after taking antidepressants and the results were almost indistinguishable.

Even if you are fortunate enough to not suffer from a common mental-health issue, learning to revise your automatic thoughts into more accurate ones will help you see the world through clearer eyes, which often makes you happier.

This isn't the "power of positive thinking," or something mystical like that. It's about the power of *accurate* thinking. Some people are prone to overly positive thinking, sure, and this process helps rein that in; most people are prone to overly negative thinking, and this process helps them be more realistically positive.

The reframing process

Let's start by rewriting the thoughts in a couple of examples that we've already seen, then we'll put it all together using some new ones.

There were two cognitive distortions present in this automatic thought: "My friend hasn't texted me back, and it's been two days. He must be mad at me. It makes sense, since he's easily offended." We identified them as jumping to conclusions and labeling.

What's a more balanced version of that automatic thought?

Here's one possible reframe: "My friend hasn't texted me back, and it's been two days. He might be mad at me, but I'd need to think about whether I've done anything to offend him. Sometimes he can be touchy, but it really depends on the situation. He might also have meant to reply, and just forgot."

Notice how the reframe didn't discount the possibility of him being angry. However, it included other possibilities as well, and thus ended up being a more accurate representation of reality—where nothing is certain.

How about: "I always feel lonely at night. I don't have enough friends." There were two thought errors: all-or-nothing thinking and emotional reasoning.

What's the more balanced thought?

A possible reframe: "I'm feeling lonely tonight. I tend to feel more lonely when it's nighttime; maybe it's just my mood fluctuating. I haven't caught up with some people in a while. I'm not extremely popular, but I do enjoy spending time with the friends I have."

Now, we can take a step back and ask, "How would thinking that make you feel?"

Probably much better than the original thought. Despite the sensation of loneliness, it's really what you make of that loneliness that has the largest influence on your mood. With a more accurate spin, it may spur you to a more productive behavior, such as reaching out to other friends.

Putting the process together

This process is called "cognitive reappraisal." The steps are:

1. Note the automatic thought and determine if it has any errors.
2. Identify what type(s) of errors are present.
3. Reframe into a more balanced thought.

Practice 1.

Your friend introduced you to someone, and after some flirtatious texting you asked if she wants to grab dinner. She replied, "Maybe." Your thought:

> Damn, that's cold. I feel like an idiot. I must have said something to turn her off. This is my problem—I always come off too strong. That's why women find me unattractive.

A. Are there any thought errors? (yes or no)
B. If so, what type(s) of thought errors?
C. Reframe into a more balanced thought.

Answer key:

A. Yes

B. Three types of thought errors:

"I *feel* like an idiot" → "I must have done something . . ."
– Emotional reasoning

"I *always* come off . . ." – All-or-nothing thinking

"women find me *unattractive*" – Labeling

Based on that thought, the resulting behaviors may include ghosting her; spending the rest of the evening moping; eating your feelings.

C. Potential reframe:
That's surprising. After all that texting, I would have expected a more enthusiastic response. Still, she may have written that response in a hurry and she may still be into it. I can try to play it cooler next time.

Resulting behaviors: following up to ask what she meant; ending up on a date with her; falling in love; getting married and living together happily ever after. (Just kidding! See skill #10 for more myths about love that set unrealistic expectations.)

This is why cognitive reappraisal is also sometimes referred to as "talking back to your inner critic." We all have an inner critic who points out our flaws. Sometimes the inner critic is right (if you never listen to it, you may never improve as a person), but often it's wrong (the inner critic is the champion of committing thought errors). You won't know unless you talk back to it—evaluate what it said and whether or not it's accurate.

Practice 2.

Your cousin told you that he voted for a different presidential candidate than you in the general election. Your thought:

I can't believe he would do that! He must really not care about the future of this country. Either he's apathetic, or he's just clueless.

A. Are there any thought errors? (yes or no)
B. If so, what type(s) of thought errors?
C. Reframe into a more balanced thought.

Answer key:

A. Yes

B. Two types of thought errors:

"He *must* not really care . . ." – Jumping to conclusions

"he's *apathetic*, or he's just *clueless*" – Labeling

Based on that thought, resulting behaviors may include further doubling down on your own righteousness; fruitless arguing about politics; resentment toward his side of the family.

C. Potential reframe:

That's surprising. He may not be as well informed as I am, or he might not value his vote as much as I do. Or, perhaps, we just disagree. He may be as passionate about this election as I am and have different viewpoints.

Resulting behaviors: keeping your cool; curiosity about his perspective. (Much more to come about navigating disagreements—including political ones—in skill #9.)

Reframing thought errors helps you treat not only yourself more fairly, but also other people. You can avoid holding them to an absurdly high standard, which will also make it easier to remain calm and keep relationships warm.

Practice 3.

Last one—a personal example without an answer key this time. Think of a time today when you felt a significant negative emotion. What were the thoughts you had that sparked that emotion?

A. Are there any thought errors? (yes or no)

B. If so, what type(s) of thought errors?

C. Reframe into a more balanced thought.

Think about how that reframed thought would have made you feel in the moment. And, how might it have led to different behavior?

Rewiring is possible

You may have noticed that many of the thoughts that contain errors come to you automatically; they can't be controlled. They are often referred to as "automatic thoughts" or "System 1 thinking" (in the behavioral-science lingo). Just as you cannot control what emotions arise in yourself, you also cannot control the thoughts that automatically come to your head. However, as we've learned, you can control how you respond to them.

Thus, I think the equation from earlier is actually more like a flowchart:

Input → automatic thought → emotion → revised thought → new emotion → behavior

That key moment after the first emotion is where you must mentally intervene.

You can make cognitive reappraisal a regular practice by keeping a "thought record" in your journal, like this:

Time of day	Negative emotion	Automatic thought	Any errors?	Type(s) of thought errors	Reframed thought

Whenever you experience a negative emotion, note it down, then go through the reappraisal process.

It may seem like a lot of work at first, but the more you practice, the easier it becomes. This process of identifying errors and reframing them gets faster and more intuitive. Eventually, it can become just as automatic as your automatic thoughts. And eventually, you'll notice that your automatic thoughts will be less riddled with thought errors. Rewiring yourself is possible—this is, in my view, one of the most powerful concepts in life (we'll come back to what I call "reprogramming your autopilot" when we tie everything together in the last chapter).

Having a partner in this thought process can help. Charlotte and I actually have a poster of the different types of thought errors framed in our bedroom—whenever one of us shares a thought that contains an error, we point it out and laugh about it.

The power of core beliefs

Some people are much more prone to thought errors than others; their thinking is typically overly negative, and often their inner critic is too loud. Why?

Cognitive psychologists have identified certain "core beliefs" we carry that color how we see almost everything—and most notably, these core beliefs are what shape our automatic thoughts (but again, not our revised thoughts, which we have control over!). Some examples of negative core beliefs:

- People cannot be trusted.
- I have to be perfect.
- I am not lovable.
- The world is a dangerous place.

As you can probably intuit, negative core beliefs are quite unhelpful. When they influence your automatic thoughts, time after time, it's easy to see how they can lead to a long-term state of depression or anxiety.

So can you change them? Guess what I'm going to say . . .

Of course! You can identify the unproductive core belief you have and determine a more productive default assumption to replace it with. For example, replacing "I am not lovable" with something like "I am worthy of being loved." Once you've determined that you would like this to be your new core belief, you can collect evidence every day that proves it is true. For example:

Core belief: I am worthy of being loved.

- I do favors for my friends—today I bought Sam lunch.
- I am kind to my boyfriend—today I helped him talk through a problem.
- I try hard to do right by others—today I told the truth even when it was very inconvenient.

Over time, the evidence in favor of the new core belief will become overwhelming. Your default way of seeing the world will have evolved to one that lifts you up rather than drags you down.

Granted, rewiring yourself at the core belief level (rather than just the automatic thoughts level) is more involved and lengthy. If you are interested in trying it, check out the recommended reading at the end of this book.[7]

Note that you can't really prove logically that a certain core belief is true or false. For example, "People cannot be trusted." Can people be trusted? Some can, and some cannot. You could spend your whole life stacking up evidence for and against this thought to determine which is "correct." It's not a matter of logic; it's a matter of perspective. A statement like "I am worthy of being loved" is not a fact—it's a choice.

---

7 Of course, some emotional problems or mental health issues require more help than a book can provide. Finding a good therapist can take work but be well worth the effort. Note that CBT is one highly evidence-backed form of therapy, but there are other useful ones as well, and different types of therapy work differently for different people.

What are your core beliefs?

The reason it takes so long to rewire core beliefs is that they are often shaped during childhood, and your mind has spent a lifetime subconsciously reinforcing them with selective observations. You cannot go back to your childhood and change how you were raised and what you internalized. (However, you can "reverse" that process using the method described above.)

For that reason, I've determined that as a parent, the most important thing I can do for my children is instill in them a set of helpful core beliefs. Here is my personal list:

1. Life is something to be excited for, not feared.
2. The world is always getting better.
3. God is benevolent.
4. People are born free, and only other people can take away that freedom.
5. People are neither good nor bad—they make decisions, and on average they are good decisions.
6. Life has meaning.
7. Your long-term fulfillment depends on helping others.
8. Your actions matter—many outcomes are determined by luck, but you can maximize your chances.
9. Your thoughts matter—your mind is always a refuge.

If you had to create your own list, what would it look like? Even if the beliefs on your list were not handed to you as a child, being able to articulate what you believe is a key facet of self-authorship (as described in skill #1), and the more you reflect and act on them, the more you will truly come to believe them.

SUMMARY

- **It's not what happens, but rather your thoughts about what happens, that impacts how you feel (and how you act).**
- **Your automatic thoughts often contain thought errors; namely, jumping to conclusions, all-or-nothing thinking, labeling, emotional reasoning.**
- **You can intercept these thoughts (and the emotions they spark) by reframing your automatic thought into a more realistic revised thought; over time, this will rewire your brain.**
- **Your automatic thoughts are shaped by your core beliefs (ways of seeing yourself and the world); any unhelpful core belief can, over time, be replaced with a more helpful one.**

Homework

Keep a thought record for one week.

Copy a version of the table from page 55 into your journal. Whenever you experience a negative emotion, write it down, then go through the reappraisal process. Ideally you will do this each time, in the moment, but whenever that's infeasible (or whenever you forget), you can also do it at one check-in point each day, like before you go to bed. Why one full week? After that time, you will likely start to notice that the process is becoming automatic.

Extra credit: Identify at least one core belief you would like to have. Add to your thought record daily any evidence that supports the belief.

II.

Financial Skills

Skill #5

BUILD CREDIT

I was raised by immigrant parents who taught me to shun debt and only spend what you have. When I was a teenager, they took me to their bank to open my first checking account; when I went to college they helped me get a debit card linked to my bank account. But never a credit card—that represented the temptation to spend too much.

For the most part, they were right—we'll talk soon about the downsides of debt and how to avoid those temptations—however, for better or worse, in today's world you need a credit card for many things.

I discovered this the hard way on the first night of my honeymoon. Charlotte and I were headed to Albuquerque (partly because we love the desert and hot-air balloons, but mostly because we love *Breaking Bad*). The flight was delayed and we arrived at eleven o'clock at night. Despite having reserved a rental car, when we got to the counter, the company wouldn't let us rent the car. Why?

"You need a credit card." Neither of us had one.

After negotiating back and forth, we learned that we could use a debit card instead. "But before swiping your debit card, we'll have to run a credit check."

Well, I failed the credit check—I'd never built credit before! It was now midnight, and the place was closing. We were stuck an hour away from our hotel in Santa Fe, on the first night of our honeymoon . . .

What's a credit score?

I promise you'll get to hear the end of the story, but first you'll need to learn some financial concepts. (I'll set all the definitions we introduce in bold so that you can come back to them as needed.)

Credit means something very simple: a loan. When your friend says, "I'm buying it on credit," she means "I'm taking a loan in order to buy it." When a bank says, "We are your **creditor**," they mean "We are the ones loaning you money." A "credit card" is called so because you get loaned money to spend during the month, and at the end of the month you have to pay back that loan.

Let's say three different people knocked on your door and asked you for a loan of $100.

1. Joe – He gives you an envelope containing three cell phone bills. You can see that for the last three months, Joe has paid his cell service provider on time.
2. Moe – He also gives you an envelope containing three cell phone bills. You can see that Moe paid his first one on time, paid the second one late, and still owes the cell service provider $50 for the last month.
3. Billy Bo – He doesn't give you an envelope. He just stares at you awkwardly.

You don't know anything else about these people, except that they each promise they'll pay you back in one month. So who would you rather give $100 credit to?

Joe makes sense, right? Joe's been paying his cell phone bill on time, so it's somewhat likely he'll pay back the loan on time.

But why should you give any of them a loan? It's your hard-earned $100, and you could use it to buy an awesome popcorn maker you found online! Let's say each of them offers to pay you **interest**. That is, after one month, they promise your $100 back plus $5 more.

An extra $5 isn't so bad! That's 5% of your $100 loan, so the monthly **interest rate** is 5%.

Now that giving credit might be worth it to you, you really want to make the right choice. How can you get more information about Joe, Moe, and Billy Bo?

You get an email from a company called Equifax saying if you pay them only $2, they can give you a ton of info: every rent, electricity, and Wi-Fi bill that Joe, Moe, and Billy Bo have received over the last two years, and whether or not they've paid them on time. Would you buy those reports?

Sure, the $2 eats into your $5 profit. But then again, if you never get back the money you've loaned, you'll lose $100. (If someone fails to pay you back, we say they **defaulted** on the loan.)

The report comes in:

1. Joe – He has often paid his electricity and Wi-Fi bills on time, but not always. He's usually paid rent on time, but he's currently late on last month.
2. Moe – He hasn't paid any bills in the last few months. His electricity's been turned off, and his landlord is threatening to evict him.
3. Billy Bo – He has paid rent, electricity, and Wi-Fi on time for the last two years. (He just doesn't save his old cell phone bills, which is why he didn't give you an envelope earlier.)

Moral of the story

In this scenario, you were playing the role of a bank. You had to decide which loan applicant was more **creditworthy**. This is also called a person's **credit risk**—the risk they won't pay back the loan you give them.

You used Equifax, which is in fact a real company, to collect more data about whether each person historically has paid things back on time. That data was delivered to you in a **credit report**.

In real life, credit reports don't usually contain the details of *every* bill you've paid. They contain some of that, but much of the information about you is combined into a **credit score**. The higher your score, the more creditworthy you probably are. Things like paying your bills on time, or having a long history of paying bills, increase your score.

The most commonly used score is called the **FICO score**. It stands for Fair Isaac Corporation, since that company invented the score in the late 1980s.

Anatomy of a credit score

The FICO score ranges from 300 ("bad") to 850 ("excellent"). It's based on five different factors. Some of these factors have more of an impact on your score than others. Here they are, ranked in order of importance:

1. Payment history – This takes into account the percentage of bills you've made on time, as well as whether or not there are any **derogatory marks** (the official term for bankruptcies, foreclosures, and any loans you didn't pay).
2. Utilization – This is the total amount of your available credit that you're using. For example, if the limit on your credit card is $5,000 and you currently have a balance of $500 (you've spent $500 this month), then your utilization is at 10%. The lower the utilization, the better—10% or less is considered good.

3. Age of credit history – The longer you've been paying off credit, the better. That's why people recommend you get your first credit card when you're young. This factor takes into account both the *average* amount of time you've had each of your credit accounts, as well as the age of the *oldest* one.
4. Mix of credit types – Besides credit cards, you may have other kinds of loans: car loans, installment loans, and mortgages. The more of these, the higher the score. That being said, it's hardly worth taking out loans that you don't need, just to bolster your score.
5. Recent inquiries – Someone who is considering you as a client or lender might make a **hard inquiry** into your credit score. Most often, these inquiries happen when you apply for a new credit card or mortgage, or submit a rent application. If you have a large number of these in the last two years, it can hurt your score. Don't confuse this with a **soft inquiry**, which doesn't affect your score at all. A soft inquiry is one that's run as part of an employee background check, preapproval for a mortgage or credit card, or your own inquiry into your credit score.

As an example, let's take a look at Billy Bo's credit report:

1. Payment history – 100% of his credit card bills have been paid on time. There are zero derogatory marks. Result: Good
2. Utilization – He has only one account, which is a credit card. That card has a limit of $10,000 and the current balance is at $1,500, so the utilization is 15%. Result: Decent
3. Age of credit history – His one credit card has only been open for nine months. Result: Bad
4. Mix of credit types – Besides the credit card, he has no other loans or credit accounts. Result: Bad
5. Recent inquiries – In the last two years, there have been two hard inquiries into his credit score (one for the credit card he now has and one for the application he submitted to rent his apartment). Result: Decent

Overall FICO score: 705 (remember, this ranges between 300 and 850).

What about all the "bad" factors in Billy Bo's credit report? As we learned, most factors don't matter nearly as much as payment history and utilization. Because his history is good and his utilization is low, that's enough to earn Billy Bo his good FICO score. He's well on his way to an "excellent" score (which is 750 and above); it just takes time to get there.

Unfortunately, I can't tell you the exact formula that is used to combine all the factors into a score—because hardly anyone knows it (it's a trade secret, protected by the Fair Isaac Corporation).

A (sadly) true story

I'm typically pretty good about paying my bills on time, but one time I ended my cell phone contract with Verizon, and they tried to charge me a cancellation fee. Feeling it was unfair, I refused to pay it, despite receiving many reminders from them. The years went on. Eventually, it turns out my unpaid bill was sold to a collection agency, who began sending me letters. "Screw them," I thought, "they're just doing Verizon's dirty work!"

You'll be proud to know I saved myself that $147. But, when Charlotte and I were ready to buy our first house, I noticed with horror that my credit report had a derogatory mark and a no-longer-pristine payment history—which reduced my credit score by at least fifty points. I tried to protest—with Verizon, with the collection agency, with the credit-reporting agencies—but to no avail.

Thankfully, Charlotte saved us by having a perfect payment history herself, which the mortgage provider was willing to use instead of my own.

I guess the moral of the story is: Always pay your bills! (But also . . . boooo Verizon.)

Why use the FICO score?

It's helpful to have this standard score as a measure of your credit worthiness so that each lender (like a landlord or a credit card company) doesn't need to have their own method of calculating it.

Lenders usually enlist the help of a **credit-reporting agency** to find out your score. The three largest agencies in the United States are TransUnion, Equifax, and Experian. They pay for information about you from banks and other sources, and combine that info into a credit report, which includes a FICO score.

The FICO score is a way of indicating how likely you are to default on (not pay back) a loan, but of course it isn't perfect. Plenty of people with high scores default on loans, and plenty of people with low scores are perfectly creditworthy. Are there better assessments of your risk? Probably. Your income, the length of time you've been able to hold down a job, your education, and many other factors might be even better indicators. I personally think you should have a higher score if you've never had a credit card, only a debit card. After all, that means you're able to pay what you owe immediately and not have to wait until the end of every month. But the question is, what information can the credit-reporting agencies access easily and cheaply? Your bank probably won't share all your debit card statements with them, but they will share your total monthly credit card bill. The agencies find the accessible information, not necessarily the best information.

Why should you care about your credit score?

If you ever need a loan, that's why! In practical terms, a higher credit score will help you to:

- Be approved for a credit card
- Pass a background check for a job application or a rent application (sometimes they check your score, sometimes they don't)
- Obtain a bank loan (if, for example, you're starting a small business)
- Get a better rate on a mortgage

That last one is the biggie. A **mortgage** is a loan to buy a house. Even if a house isn't top of mind for you now, it may be eventually. (However, contrary to conventional wisdom, it's not necessarily a good investment for everyone! More on that in skill #8.) A few years ago the national average interest rate for a thirty-year loan (a loan you must pay off within thirty years) was 3.2% if your FICO score was 760 or higher, but it was 4.8% if your FICO score was 640 or lower.

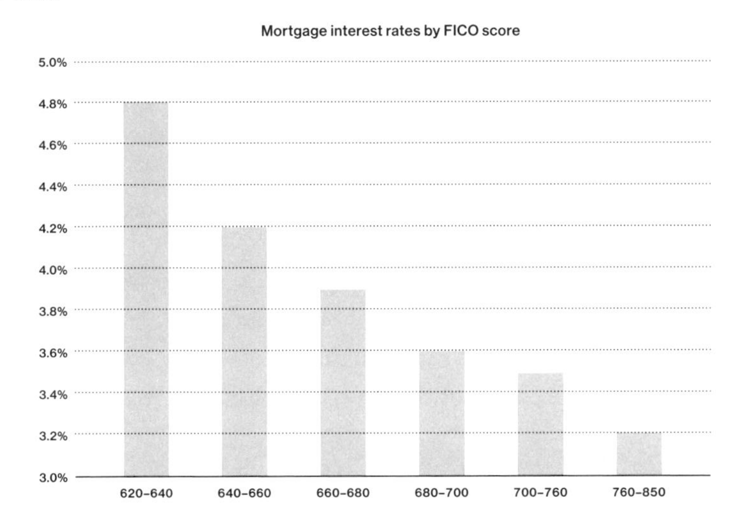

You may be thinking, "What's the big deal? How much of a difference could there even be between an 4.8% and a 3.2% interest rate?"

The answer is: a lot. Let's say you take out a thirty-year mortgage on a house that costs $400,000. The difference in how much you will pay over the lifetime of the loan is between $560,000 and $680,000—that's $120,000 of your money!

Why should you *not* care about your credit score?

While it can make a big difference in the amount you pay for interest on your home, your credit score isn't the be-all and end-all of personal finance. Many people out there will try to convince you that you should always be thinking about your credit score, particularly when they're trying to get you to buy something from them—like a loan or a credit card.

What matters more?

Well, your money. Decisions that impact your credit score should matter to you only to the extent that they affect your money. So, knowing how a different credit score will affect your interest rate is important. But so is your salary—for example, if you got a raise of $3,000, it would more than make up for the more expensive mortgage over those thirty years.

We'll see a similar concept play out in the next chapter, which covers investing. Optimizing investments is important to some extent, but unless you are very wealthy, it's typically much better to spend your time optimizing your salary and lowering your expenses.

With that disclaimer, we can move on to the number one way to **build credit** (increase your credit score over time): credit cards. To illustrate a central principle of credit cards, we'll start with . . .

How credit cards work

Don't confuse credit cards with debit cards. A **debit card** is a card you usually get with a checking account. When you spend with it, or use it to withdraw money from an ATM, the money is immediately deducted from your account.

When you use a **credit card**, you're essentially taking a loan from the credit card company. There are actually two ways to pay back that loan:

1. Monthly – Each month, you can spend up to your **credit limit**. At the end of the month you must pay back that loan (you don't have to pay any interest on it).

2. Inter-month – If you don't pay back the loan, your **balance carries** to the next month. That means you still owe it, but now interest has begun to accrue.

There is no such thing as free money! Credit cards, like any loan, obey the law of financial gravity: Whatever is borrowed must be paid back—with interest.

As an example, let's say the credit limit on your card is $1,000. You spend $850 over the course of the month. At the end of the month, you get a bill for how much? $850. You're paying it off fully, so there's no interest—thus $850 is the total you owe.

Now, let's say you only pay $800 at the end of the month. How much will you owe in the future? The $50 is your balance, which carries to the next month, so you owe interest on it.

How much interest, exactly?

Annual percentage rate

Each credit card has an **annual percentage rate**, abbreviated **APR**, that tells you how much interest you will owe if you let your balance carry. Most credit card APRs are somewhere between 10% and 40%.

Let's say your APR is 12% (a pretty typical rate). Each month, you will have to pay 1% interest—because that's 12% divided by twelve months. That means if you let your balance carry for a year, you'll end up owing your original balance plus 12.7% of it.

Wait, why 12.7%, not 12%?

Aha! You've spotted one of the financial industry's sneaky tricks. The APR doesn't take compounding into account. Although you'd think *annual* percentage rate would be a yearly figure, you actually owe interest each month. You owe 1% interest each month, and after the first month, you start owing interest on the interest. So, by the end of the year, it's increased by 1% a total of twelve times, which comes out to 12.7%. An APR of 20% actually comes out to about 22% per year, and 40% is really 48% per year!

How much is this in actual dollars? Let's say at the end of January, you pay all of your credit card bill except for $500 of it. You let that $500 balance continue to carry over each month, on a credit card with a 12% APR. At the end of the year, you'd owe $563. Ten years later, your innocent $500 has become a debt of $1,650—over three times as much! And, of course, all of this assumes that the APR stays constant each month. In many cases, though, the APR has a tendency to increase because of:

- **Variable rates:** "Variable" just means that the credit card company can change the APR. In many cases, it increases if your credit score goes down. But it can also increase for a variety of other reasons—sometimes unexpectedly.
- **Introductory rates:** Some cards will have a 0% APR introductory rate for the first year. But after that, the APR bumps up to a normal amount. (That means that any balance you have will start to accrue interest after the first year.) "Introductory" is a nice euphemism—most people call it by its more accurate name: a teaser rate.

There's one more quirk about an APR. I know I said you don't owe any interest on your balance as long as you pay it off by the end of the month. But if you let any balance carry over, even $1, you'll end up owing interest even on what you did pay.

That's because your interest is based on your **average daily balance**. In our example, you paid off $800 of your $850 bill, and let $50 carry. Now you'll owe interest on the average balance each day in that month. So if, on average during that past month, you had $500 total charged to your card, you'll owe interest on $500, not just $50. Pretty sneaky!

Credit card companies do not give you free money; they give you a loan. And if you don't pay back the full amount of that loan at the end of every month, interest will accumulate. Eventually, you will have to pay it back—sometimes, as we saw, it can grow up to three times as much as what you borrowed. The law of financial gravity is as true for credit cards as for anything else.

There's a simple way to avoid all the complexity of compounding APR, teaser rates, and average daily balances . . .

Paying your balance

Be careful not to confuse paying your balance with paying your **minimum payment**. Most credit cards have a minimum payment of about $35 (which may go up over time). All this means is that if you don't pay at least $35 of your balance each month, you'll owe a penalty fee in addition to the interest. And your credit score will be dinged.

Remember the most important factor in your FICO score? (Payment history!) One of the worst ways you can hurt your score is by not meeting the minimum payments on your credit card—it can knock up to 75 points from your score, and it can linger on your credit report for up to seven years. (Seven years is a long time!) But if you make the minimum payment yet still have even $1 of your balance unpaid, you'll start owing interest.

That's why, once you have a credit card, you should set up **auto-pay**. It's the best way to make sure you remember to pay your bill at the end of each month—because you don't even have to remember. It will automatically deduct a set amount from your bank account (that you link to) to pay your balance before the due date. You can either have it pay the minimum payment (typically $35), a fixed amount (like $100), or automatically pay the full balance (definitely the best option!). Since it will deduct this amount from your bank account, be sure you have enough in your bank account to cover the payment.

Credit card billing statements can be confusing. Up until now, we've been saying that you're billed at the end of each month. Really, there's a **billing cycle**, which is one month long, but these rarely line up with the first and last days of the calendar month (for example, March 20 to April 19). At the end of the billing cycle, your balance closes, and you must pay it, unless you want it to carry over and start accruing interest. Usually you have about three weeks after the statement closes until your **due date**, which is when you have to make the actual payment.

The end of each billing cycle isn't the only time you should check your credit card statement. The statement is basically a bill that shows you all of the charges on your card. It's a good idea to check it online at least once a week, to make sure that there's nothing fishy going on. It's possible you'll find a fraudulent charge, or someone who billed you by accident. Once, I saw that a restaurant charged me twice for the same meal. If I hadn't checked the credit card statement, I never would have known to call the restaurant and ask for a refund. Since then, I check my credit card statement every Sunday night.

Okay, you get it. Credit cards should be used as a convenient substitute for cash, not as a supplement to your income. At this point, you might be wondering, "Isn't it easier to avoid credit cards altogether? Why not just stick with a debit card?"

Benefits of having a credit card

1. Building your credit score – As long as you pay your full balance each month, you'll see your FICO score increase steadily. And as we learned before, having a good credit score can save you tens (or even hundreds) of thousands of dollars by getting you a lower mortgage rate.

Remember that your credit score also increases if you have lower utilization (if you only spend a small percentage of the credit available to you). So if you want to increase your score further, you can raise your credit limit. Usually you can do this with an online form, and otherwise you can call—you'd be surprised how often they just say yes!

And in addition to setting up autopay, you can pay off your balance more frequently, to keep your utilization number as low as possible.

FAQ: But don't you need to already have a good credit score in order to get a credit card in the first place?

Pretty much. So how do you get yourself out of the catch-22? Not all credit cards require a high score; sometimes showing that you have a regular income is enough to be approved. There are certain types of cards that don't require any credit history at all (we'll go over some options at the end of the chapter).

2. Rewards system – Many credit cards offer "rewards" for using them on purchases. These come in the form of points (which can be spent like cash at some stores), airline miles, hotel points, or even cash. For most cards, the reward ends up being worth about 1% of what you spend. So if you spend $10,000 on your credit card in a year, you get about $100 in rewards. It's a nice perk, but not a game-changer.

3. Disputing charges – Whether a store has charged you twice by accident, or there is fraudulent activity on your card, you can **dispute** the charge (refuse to pay it). With a debit card, the money leaves your account immediately; but with a credit card, you

haven't technically given up your money yet (you owe it to the credit card company at the monthly due date), so they take responsibility for recovering it from the merchant. Debit cards will also usually help you through these situations; it's just that credit card companies are known for making it a bit easier.

4. Car-rental insurance – Many credit cards include a type of insurance that covers damage to rental cars.

5. Borrowing money – Some people see the ability to borrow money for a month as the main benefit of credit cards. Of course, we're now intimately familiar with its dangers. But it *can* be useful in some situations. For example, if you've just graduated from college and need money for moving expenses before you get your first paycheck. Just be sure you will be able to pay your balance at the end of the month.

So, is it worth taking out *multiple* credit cards? Generally, having more credit cards is a good thing for your credit score, to lower utilization (since you'll have a higher total credit limit). But is it really worth the hassle of having another account you need to manage and having another bill to pay? Missing even one monthly payment accidentally will hurt your score a lot more than having that extra account helps it. As long as you trust yourself to turn on autopay, and to monitor the account occasionally, you can open more cards to raise your credit score, or to benefit from the various point schemes. (For example, my wife and I have an Amazon credit card through Chase that gives 5% back on Amazon purchases, so we only use it for that purpose.)

What about closing old credit cards? Doing so will lower your credit score in two ways. Temporarily, it will hurt your "age of credit history" factor. More importantly, it will worsen your utilization score because it's one more credit limit you no longer have. For example, if you have two cards, each with a $1,000 limit, and you spend an average of $100 per month, your utilization would be around 5% previously ($100 divided by $2,000); but after closing a card, it would go up to 10%. As always, it's a cost-benefit analysis: If you can trust yourself to stay on top of that card, keep it; otherwise, close it.

FAQ: How do credit card companies make money?

Their main source of revenue is interchange fees. Every time you swipe your credit card at a restaurant or a store (whether in person or online), that merchant is charged a fee. Usually it's about 2.7% of what you paid. (Now you know why some restaurants don't take credit cards.) Of course, the credit card companies also make money whenever you pay them interest on your debt.

So shouldn't they want to get customers with *bad* credit scores? It's true that a bad credit score might indicate that the person won't pay on time, so their balance will accrue interest. However, the possibility of more revenue from interest just isn't worth the risk that the customer will never pay what they owe. When someone defaults on their loans, the lender has to hire a collection agency to try to get their money back, but it's expensive—and a customer could declare bankruptcy (which eliminates many of their debts).

Credit card companies want people with good credit scores so badly that they're willing to entice them by offering them cards with lower APRs. (Ironically, lower APRs don't matter to the kinds of people who always pay their balance on time.)

The burden of consumer debt

The availability of loans, in the form of things like credit cards, makes it all too easy to rationalize getting into (or being in) debt. Of course, there are many different types of debt, some of which people call "good" debt (like student debt or mortgages). I'd personally dispute that term, but I don't think that anyone would dispute that **consumer debt** (credit card debt being the primary kind) is "bad" debt—because the interest rates are so high.

Have you ever found yourself thinking one of these thoughts?

> I already spent so much this month, spending a little more won't make a difference.

Of course it will make a difference! There's no point beating yourself up over having spent a lot of money. The best thing you can do (which will also make you feel better about yourself) is just to spend less going forward.

> There's no point of saving money since my debt just eats up my savings.

That's exactly why you should save money! Using what you've saved each month to pay off debt isn't a waste of money at all—it's a great use of money.

> I'm already in debt, so borrowing more won't make a difference.

It will make a very big difference. The more debt you have, the longer it will take to pay it back—and because interest compounds, the amount you owe will increase faster and faster the longer you owe it. Each additional $1 you borrow while in debt will end up costing you much more than $1.

FAQ: What if I already have a credit card, and I'm deep in consumer debt?

If so, I'm sorry. I know being in debt is hard, and it can feel like things are out of your control. I hope reading this chapter didn't feel too much like rubbing salt in your wounds. But, you don't have to label yourself as "the type of person who doesn't pay their balance" forever. Unless you have other, more pressing debts, paying off your credit card balance is probably the best use of your money right now.

Let's say your friend, who's been carrying a balance of $1,000 on their credit card, was just pleasantly surprised by a bonus at work. They say, "I can always use my regular paycheck to pay back that debt. I should use the bonus to treat myself to something fun, like a flat-screen TV."

What would you tell them?

Here's one possible answer: "There's no real difference between income (that you were expecting) and a bonus (that was a pleasant surprise). It's all your money, and you can choose how to spend it. It would be great to have a flat-screen TV now, but unfortunately the longer the credit card debt lingers, the more you'll owe. Paying it back now will feel so good—you'll be treating yourself in a different way!"

A happy ending

Because I didn't know all this, Charlotte and I were stuck at the Albuquerque airport on the first night of our honeymoon, nearing the midnight closing time for the car-rental desks, with no car.

Thankfully, after trying multiple rental agencies there, the lady at one was incredibly kind and agreed to let us rent using my debit card without a credit check (by placing a hefty deposit on it). She felt so bad that she upgraded us to a pickup truck so that (and I quote): "You can drive out into the desert and use the flatbed to do your honeymoon business."

When we got home after the trip, we both applied for credit cards. And thus began our lives as adults together.

SUMMARY

- **Your FICO score is a standardized measure of your creditworthiness; its main purpose is to give lenders an idea of how much risk there is that you won't pay back their loan.**
- **The most important factors in your FICO score are your payment history (paying your bills on time) and your utilization rate (not using all the credit that's available to you).**
- **Having a good credit score is useful for getting loans and lower interest rates on large purchases such as a house.**
- **Credit cards are great for building up your credit score, but remember the law of financial gravity: "Whatever is borrowed must be paid back—with interest."**
- **Paying off your credit card in full each month is the only way to avoid paying interest (which has a tendency to grow huge); set up autopay and consider paying the full balance even more frequently than monthly in order to keep your utilization low.**

Homework

First, check your credit score—both so you can understand these concepts better, and so you can make sure there are no errors in it.

You have two good options:

1. By law, you're entitled to one free credit report per year from Equifax, Experian, and TransUnion. You can fill out some info to request these reports at www.annualcreditreport.com.
2. Alternatively, there are services that use soft inquiries to get your FICO score every month from Equifax, Experian, and TransUnion. I personally find Credit Karma really convenient. (Beware, though, of all the other features on the site. They'll try to get you to sign up for credit cards and loans that are "tailored" to the info you supplied—in reality, it's advertising that certain cards pay to have shown.)

Second, if you don't already have a credit card, get one! There are credit cards that are particularly suited for people with bad credit or little credit history. Meaning, they're not that great—they might have a high APR and few perks. But those things don't matter nearly as much as the ability to start somewhere. Search online and see if you can find a credit card that has a decent chance of accepting your application. If you're having a hard time getting a credit card, you can try your bank. Most banks will offer you their own credit card because you're already a customer.

If even your bank won't approve your credit card application, ask them for a "secured card." These have an annual fee (usually around $50) and a low credit limit—not ideal. But you can hold onto it long enough to build up your credit score, then close the account once you've been approved for a better credit card. (Charlotte, who was in medical school with no income, got her start with a secured card—it was a pain, but over time she built enough credit to get a real credit card, and eventually her credit score surpassed mine!)

Once you get a credit card (or if you already have one), you have two missions:

1. Set up autopay—and set it to pay off the full balance of the credit card each billing cycle.
2. Set yourself a weekly recurring calendar invite to check your credit card balance and make sure there's nothing fishy on the statement (and that you're not getting too close to your credit limit).

Extra credit: Call your credit card company and ask for a credit-limit increase, in order to lower your utilization percentage (*not* so you can spend more money!). You'll be surprised how often they say yes.

Skill #6

INVEST YOUR MONEY

In my first year after college, I learned two startling facts.

First, in order to be able to afford to retire at an old age, you need to save *a lot* of money. Social Security—the 6.2% tax we pay from every paycheck (in addition to income tax)—pays people who are currently retired. However, it only pays an average of $21,000 per year to folks over sixty-five, which is not enough for most people to live on. Worse, Social Security is a kind of pyramid scheme, wherein the people working today pay for the people who are retired today, so each generation must be at least as large as the previous one—a trend that is not guaranteed to continue. By the time you and I are retired, we will likely be receiving much less than $21,000, possibly even $0.

Second, you need to save *even more than a lot* of money for retirement because of inflation. Inflation (rising prices) varies from year to year, but it has averaged 3.7% per year over the past sixtyish years. That means that your $100 will be worth about $96 next year (you can buy $96 worth of stuff with it); in five years it will be worth about $83; and when you retire in forty years, it will be worth only $22.

So, let's say you plan to retire at age sixty-five and expect to live for thirty more years after that. Assuming you own your own home by then, and don't have large medical expenses that Medicare won't cover—both of which are big assumptions—you'll probably want to spend about $30,000 per year. That means you'll need $30,000 x 30 years = $900,000 saved up. Because of inflation, that means you'll need to save *over $4 million* in today's dollars. (In forty years, today's $4 million will likely only be able to buy you $900,000 worth of stuff.)

I couldn't believe nobody had taught me these facts before! Shouldn't we know, from the time we begin our careers, that we must be saving money for retirement?

The good news

Actually, you need to save a lot less than $4 million, because of investing.

Investing is about putting your money to work. In financial terms, investing means saving money in a way that will *earn* you money. If you've ever earned interest in a bank account, then you've invested! You saved your money there, and those savings earned you more money (in interest that the bank paid you). Besides bank accounts, there are plenty of other ways to invest. Two of the most common ones are stocks and bonds, which we'll learn about soon.

Note: The purpose of this chapter is primarily to teach you about how to invest for retirement, although we will cover some shorter-term investment principles as well. In order to reach our final, important conclusions, we first need to cover some essential basics.

Using what you learn in this chapter, it's reasonable to expect your investments to return 9% per year (meaning, the money you invest will increase by 9% per year). At that rate, how much will you have in the future? Invested now, in forty years, $10,000 will become $314,000.

Wait, what? That's more than thirty-one times as much! Even after we take inflation into account, it will be worth over $93,000—over nine times as much. (This is also excluding taxes, which eat a chunk of your growth. We'll get into taxes in more detail soon.)

How? The same principle that makes inflation so scary is also what makes investing so powerful . . .

The wonder of compounding

Let's say you have an egg. Instead of cracking it open, you incubate it. The egg hatches into a chicken. Then, the chicken lays ten eggs. Now you have nine more eggs than you started with. Instead of cracking them open, you fertilize each of those eggs so they hatch into chickens. If those chickens each lay ten eggs, how many eggs will you have? One hundred.

Let's do another example, this time in dollars. Say you have $100, and it grows at 10% per year (which is a more realistic growth rate for money than the 100% growth rate for the chickens). How much do you have after the first year? $110. Now your $110 grows by 10% again, so you have how much at the end of the second year? $120?

No! You have a bit more than that. Actually, you're earning 10% of *$110*, which is $11. At the end of the second year you have $110 plus $11, for a total of $121.

The amount you earn in the second year ($11) is more than the amount you earned in the first year ($10). Each year, the percentage growth stays the same, but the amount you have that's growing is higher. So, you earn more each year than you earned the previous year. (At the end of the third year, you'd have $133. After ten years, you'd have $260.)

Compounding is also called **compound growth**—it's something growing at the same percentage each year, so it gets bigger faster and faster.

Let's see exactly how fast compound growth happens. Take a look at the graph:

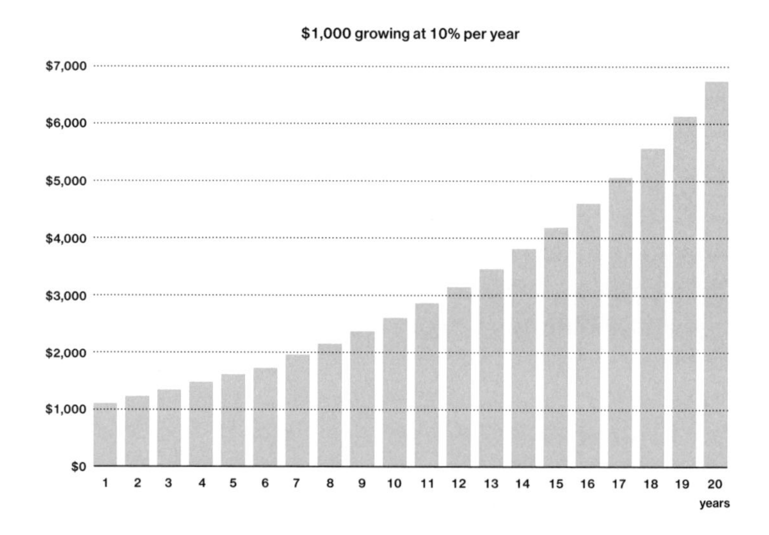

Notice the upward curve? That's because the height difference between each bar gets bigger and bigger over time—because the money is growing faster each year than it did in the previous year.[8]

Okay, that's enough about compounding. We can now move on to—

[8] In case you're curious, the formula I used to generate this graph—the formula for compound growth—is *P*(1+r)^y* (P is your principal, or starting amount; r is the rate of growth, in this case 9%; y is the number of years).[9]

[9] A footnote within a footnote? What is this, witchcraft? (It's not as witchcraft-y as the magic of compounding!) There's a mental math trick to do this formula in your head, called "The Rule of 72." If you know that something grows by a certain percentage each year, you can divide 72 by that number to see how long it takes to double. For example, if your money grows by 9% each year, you calculate 72 / 9 = 8. That means every eight years, your money doubles. After the first eight years you'll have twice as much as you started with; after another eight years you'll have four times as much as you started with; and so on. (This is more of a trick than a rule, since the numbers aren't totally precise. But for basic calculations in your head, it's a great shortcut.)

Just kidding!

Actually, I'm still not over compounding. It's amazing!

You may notice this feels a lot like APR (credit card interest rates) . . . That's because it's the same. APR compounds, too. It actually compounds every month rather than every year, which is why it grows even faster.

Any growth that's written as a percentage compounds. We saw how powerful this growth is when it works in our favor—but it can work against you, too. If you owe money, the interest grows faster and faster. Albert Einstein is quoted as saying, "Compound interest is the eighth wonder of the world. He who understands it, earns it. He who doesn't, pays it."[10]

I also want to emphasize how important timing is. The earlier you invest, the more time your money has to grow. The money that you invest for retirement now will be worth so much more than the money you invest when you're close to retirement. If you invest $5,000 for forty years, it will likely be worth more than twenty times as much as it would if you only invested it five years away from retirement.

So, even though the end of your working life may feel a long way off, it's so much better to start investing now. You might miss the $5,000 this year, but you'll appreciate the $157,000 when your days are full of beaches and margaritas.

Compounding is the most important principle of investing. Now, we can start learning about the actual investments you can make, starting with . . .

---

10 People dispute whether Einstein actually said this. Perhaps the quote was misattributed but shared with a few people, who shared it with more people—compounding all over the internet!

Stocks

One day, Emily invents a new program to organize emails. Other people want to buy the program, so she starts her own company: *E-maily*. As the program's sales increase, so do the company's profits. After one year, E-maily is worth $1,000.

Emily created the whole company herself, so she owns 100% of it. But she doesn't have $1,000 in her bank account—that's the company's theoretical value. What if Emily wants cash for herself?

Kelly, an investor, is willing to buy a piece of the company. Emily sells 10% of the company for $100. Now 10% of E-maily is owned by Kelly, and the remaining 90% is owned by Emily.

Emily is $100 richer. What was in it for Kelly? Kelly bought her piece because she believed in the company. And true to her faith, E-maily continues to do well—everyone wants their emails organized! After another year, E-maily is worth $1,300. So Kelly's 10% is worth $130.

Shellie, another investor, wants in on the action. She buys Kelly's piece for $130, so Kelly walks away with a $30 profit.

Kelly made $30 by buying and then selling a **stock**. A stock is a piece of a company. When the company's value increases, so does the stock. You can share in a company's success! (A stock is also called a **share**.) The price of each share is the total value of the company divided by the number of shares that exist.

The stock market isn't a place, it's a concept. People buy and sell stocks all the time. Companies whose stock is up for trade are called **public companies**. You've heard of public companies; they include Apple, Coca-Cola, Amazon, and Walmart, among many others. (When their stocks are traded, their names often get abbreviated to use as their ticker symbols: AAPL, KO, AMZN, WMT.)

By contrast, **private companies** are owned by a small group of people. It's not that these people don't want to cash out on their shares—sometimes they do sell them. They just don't make them publicly available to the highest bidder. Plenty of big companies choose to remain private. (My personal favorite: The LEGO Group.)

Anyone can invest in stocks, but the actual nitty-gritty buying and selling is done by **stockbrokers**. Nowadays, many brokers offer their services via online companies like E-Trade or Robinhood. The actual stocks change hands via a place called a **stock exchange**.[11]

There are two ways to earn returns (money) from buying and selling stocks:

1. Capital gains – **Capital gains** is just a fancy word for profit. It means you've earned more than what you paid on an investment. We already saw an example of this. When Kelly sold her share of E-maily, she made $30 in capital gains.

2. Dividends – Some companies pay their shareholders (the people who own their stock) every once in a while. These payments are called **dividends**. Different companies pay dividends at different times, but many happen quarterly (four times per year). The amounts also range, but they usually average around 1.5% of the value of the stock per year.

FAQ: Why would a company want to pay dividends?
They do so to reward their shareholders, which makes more people want to own their shares, which drives their stock price up. Other companies, such as Amazon, say they will never pay dividends because they'd rather use that money to increase the value of the company in other ways, such as spending it on research and development.

[11] If you're picturing people yelling and holding up little slips of paper, you're thinking of a physical stock exchange such as the New York Stock Exchange. Walmart (WMT) and Coca-Cola (KO) shares are traded there, along with almost two thousand other public companies. Other exchanges, like the Nasdaq, are purely virtual. Apple (AAPL) and Amazon (AMZN) shares trade hands digitally, along with over three thousand other public companies in the Nasdaq. There are plenty of other stock exchanges in the United States, and most other countries have at least one as well. As an ordinary investor, the exchange that your stocks are traded in typically doesn't make any difference to you.

Bonds

E-maily has more customers than ever, but some of them are complaining that the program crashes frequently. E-maily doesn't yet make enough profit to upgrade their servers, so they need to take out a loan. Kelly agrees to lend $1,000 of her own money to E-maily. E-maily promises to pay Kelly's $1,000 back in five years. In the meantime, E-maily will keep Kelly happy by paying her $40 each year.

But after only three years, Kelly's car bites the dust and she needs cash to buy a new one. She can't wait another two years to get her $1,000 back from E-maily. Once again, Shellie wants to get in on the moneymaking action. She offers to buy the loan from Kelly for $1,000. In this case, it's a win-win: Kelly gets her $1,000 back now, and Shellie holds on to the loan for another two years, getting paid $40 from E-maily each year.

The loan that Kelly made (and later sold to Shellie) is a **bond**: a loan to a company, or a government. When companies or governments need cash, they issue bonds (they ask people for loans). Like stocks, bonds can be bought and sold. Whoever owns the bond at its **maturity date** (the last day of the loan) gets paid back by the company or government.

How is this different from a stock? Note that in the first story, Emily sold a piece of her ownership in the company to Kelly so that Emily could get cash for herself. In the second story, Emily didn't sell any ownership—she personally still owns 90% of the company. Instead, E-maily (the company itself) borrowed money from Kelly, and later paid back that money to Shellie (the new owner of the loan).

Owners of a bond earn money from:

3. Interest – In our example, the E-maily bond paid 4% **interest** per year (since they paid $40 each year, on a loan of $1,000).

Of course, there's no guarantee that the owner of a bond will be paid back. Just like individual borrowers, companies (or even governments) can **default** on the bond (not be able to pay it back).

And stocks, just like bonds, have risk. Not only the risk that they won't grow as fast as you expected—but also the risk that they'll decrease in value. When a stock you own decreases below the original price you paid for it, you've actually lost money overall, so it's called a **capital loss**.

The volatility of the stock market

Stock prices go up and down all the time, even on a daily basis. Here's Walmart's stock price over the course of one day:

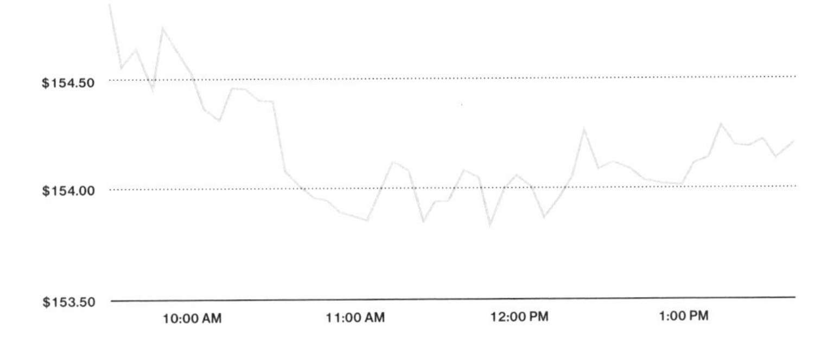

And here's Walmart's stock price over the course of five years:

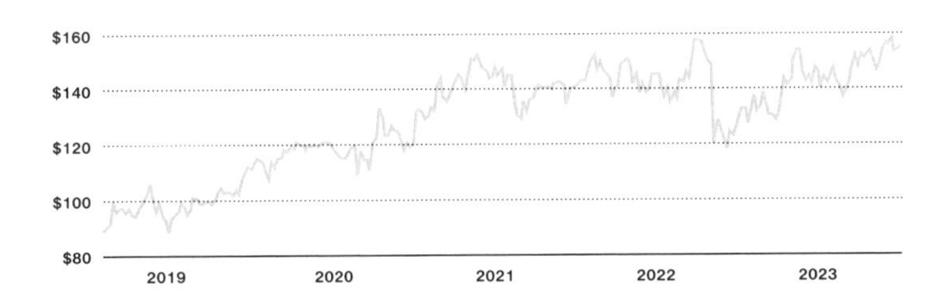

Even though Walmart's stock price is higher than it was before, it's been a bumpy road. If you had bought one share five years ago and sold it on the last day of that chart, you'd have made a profit. But if you had bought that share one-and-a-half years ago, you'd have lost a bit of money. This short-term bumpiness is called **volatility**.

In our story, Kelly made $30 off E-maily stock. Was she an employee of E-maily? No. Did she have to do any work? Nope! All she had to do was buy the share. But Kelly did have to take on some risk. In the end, she sold the stock at the right time—she got lucky.

Stock prices are unpredictable. It's impossible to know what the price will be tomorrow, let alone five years in the future. If you sell now, the stock might go up even more tomorrow. If you wait until tomorrow to sell, it might tank by then.

But here's the key: Even though stocks jump around seemingly randomly, and some even totally crash (if a company goes broke), on average stocks tend to increase in value.

How do we know this? By adding up the value of the total stock market—all United States public companies' stocks added together—and looking at its price over time.

On any given day, the total stock market appears just as erratic as an individual stock. But over long periods of time, it's clear that it tends to increase. Here's the total stock market over the last forty years (from 1983 to 2023):

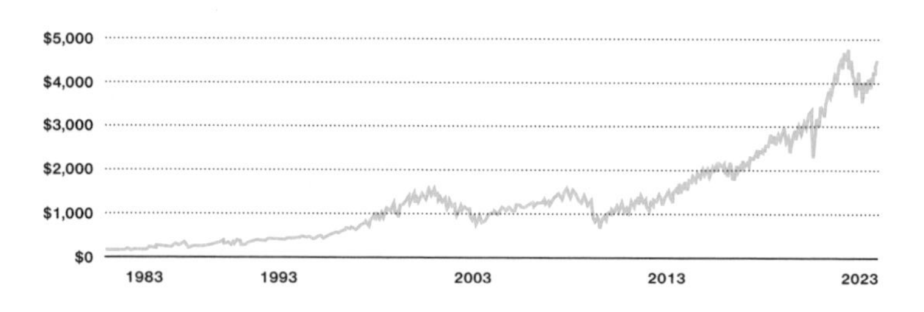

II. FINANCIAL SKILLS

And here it is over the last 150 years:

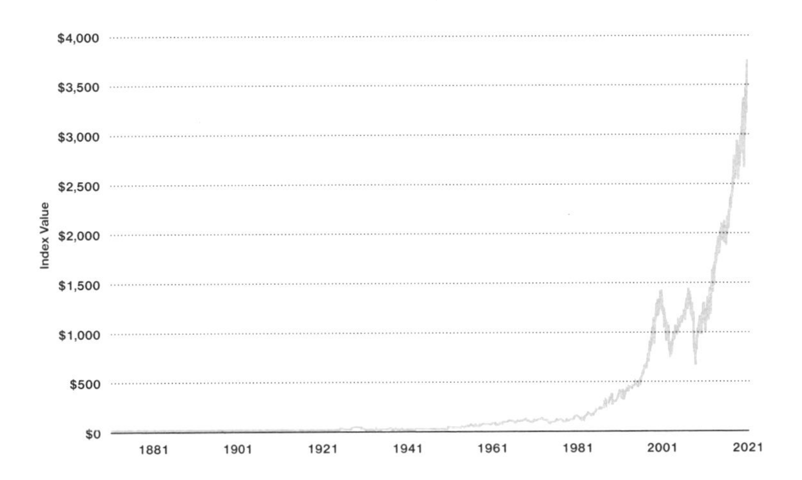

If you had invested $1 in the total stock market in 1870, and withdrew it in 2023, you'd have over $300,000!

Quick note: Oftentimes, we'll refer to "the total stock market" interchangeably with "the S&P 500," which is an index (weighted list) of the five hundred largest companies in the United States,[12] tracked by the firm Standard & Poor's. In 2024, the value of these five hundred companies accounted for $43 trillion out of the $51 trillion in total value of the US stock market, and their trajectory matched almost exactly.

So how does the total stock market work its magic? It benefits from a simple but awesome idea . . .

---

12 You may have heard of other indexes like the Nasdaq (which tracks all stocks listed on the Nasdaq exchange) or the Dow Jones Industrial Average (which tracks thirty large companies). There can also be indexes that track other things, such as medium-size companies in China (by containing a small representative group of medium-size companies in China). There can even be indexes for bonds.

Diversification

Let's look at two hypothetical companies:

- Coats & Co. sells a lot of coats every year, but it sells even more when winter goes long.
- Lemon Drink, Inc. sells a lot of lemonade every year, but it sells even more when winter is short and spring comes early.

So what happens if you own stock in both? Whether the groundhog sees its shadow or not, you're safe. A long winter means a higher Coats & Co. stock price, and a short winter means a higher Lemon Drink, Inc. stock price. Both companies will grow, but one will grow more than the other. By having both, you benefit from the *average* growth between the two. In this way, your investments are **diversified**.

But why does the total stock market tend to increase overall, instead of averaging 0%? Over time, the country becomes more prosperous. The work that people do generates money, and a good amount of this money is in the value of public companies—which you can invest in by buying their stock.

Professional gamblers

Of course, you don't have to trade individual stocks yourself. There are plenty of people who are willing to do it for you—in exchange for a fee. But because everyone is trading in the same stock market, for every investment advisor who gets higher returns than the average, another must get lower returns than the average. So 50% of all investment advisors will lose ("lose" meaning do worse than the average—that is, the total stock market).

And even among the "winners," you still have to pay the fee. Therefore, having someone else trade stocks for you will lose you money on average.

"On average" is one thing. But do you think you can pick an investment advisor who is better than average at trading stocks? Sometimes you can, and sometimes you can't—at least half the time you will be wrong. The movement of stocks is impossible to predict; they behave randomly, according to a pattern called a "random walk."[13] Stock traders are making guesses. The *Wall Street Journal* used to host a competition pitting stock traders against people randomly throwing darts at a board—and the winners were usually a mix of the two types of people.

Many traders, though, still claim that they're better than the average. In fact, you've probably seen advertisements for investment advisors who claim they can beat the total stock market. Or perhaps you have a friend who made it big trading stocks.

Of course, you're more likely to hear from the winners than from the losers. Why would the losers want to flaunt their losses? Furthermore, the successful ones frequently attribute their success to skill rather than luck. That's called **results-oriented thinking**.

For example, let's say I offered you a bet. You will roll a dice, and if you get a six, you win $1,000. But if you roll any other number, you have to pay me $1,000.

You take the bet, and give the dice a spin . . . You get a six. You won $1,000!

Given that you won, do you think it was a good bet? Of course not. You had a one in six chance of winning, but a five in six chance of losing. The fact that you won doesn't change that. You happened to get lucky, but it was still a bad decision. Five out of every six times that you took the bet, you would lose $1,000.

There are numerous studies showing that, similarly, when it comes to the performance of stock pickers or fund managers, past performance is no indication of future performance. If someone beats the average one year, it is not any more likely they will beat it

---

13 This pattern, also called Brownian motion, was first observed in the movement of pollen grains in water; Albert Einstein later explained the theory behind it. And in the 1990s, two economists won a Nobel Prize for showing how it applies to the stock market.

the next year. If someone beats the average for five years in a row (which does happen, by chance), their chances of beating the average the next year are still no greater than anyone else's.[14]

The stock market is like a casino stapled to a money tree. The key is to plant your money tree and let it grow while avoiding the slot machines in the casino. Picking stocks (or funds, wherein others manage your stocks) is similar to gambling; investing itself is not gambling. The consistent growth of the total stock market can almost always be relied upon—when it comes to the total stock market, long-term past performance *is* an indication of long-term future performance.

What do I mean by that? Yes, the total stock market is volatile day to day, even year to year. But over a long stretch of time—based on over 150 years of recorded evidence—it has always gone up. This is a crucial point, so we'll dive in further, with plenty of charts to illustrate it.

The long-term bands of the total stock market

On a day-to-day basis, the total stock market can certainly be volatile. Similarly, over the course of one year, there can be a big range of returns. During some years, the total stock market grows a lot. Historically, it can increase by up to 55% in one year! That happened in 1933.

---

14 There are some possible exceptions, among certain hedge funds and private equity funds. Generally, these funds are not available to retail investors (an average person), but only to large institutions or ultra-wealthy people.

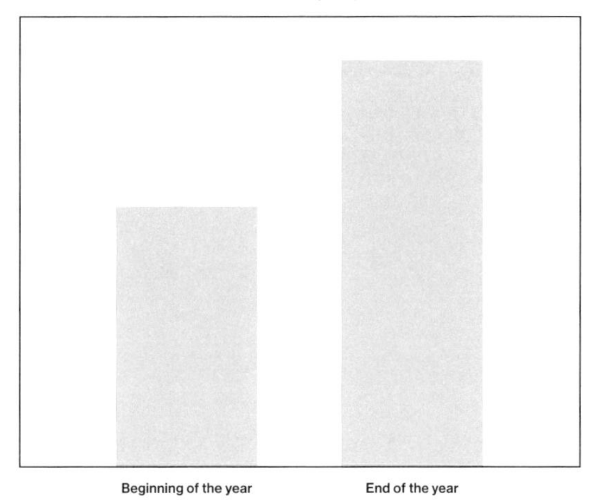

Other years, it loses value. Historically, it can decrease by almost 43% in one year. That happened in 1931.

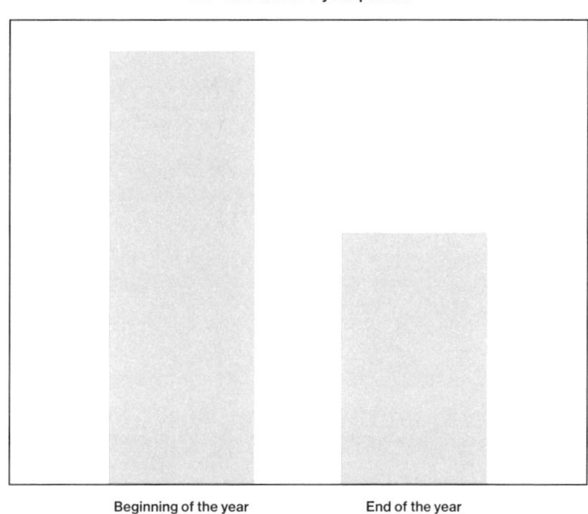

What happens over a five-year period? If you invest money in the total stock market, and don't touch it until five years later, then in the *best case* it could grow by 28% per year (on average). That happened from 1924 to 1929.

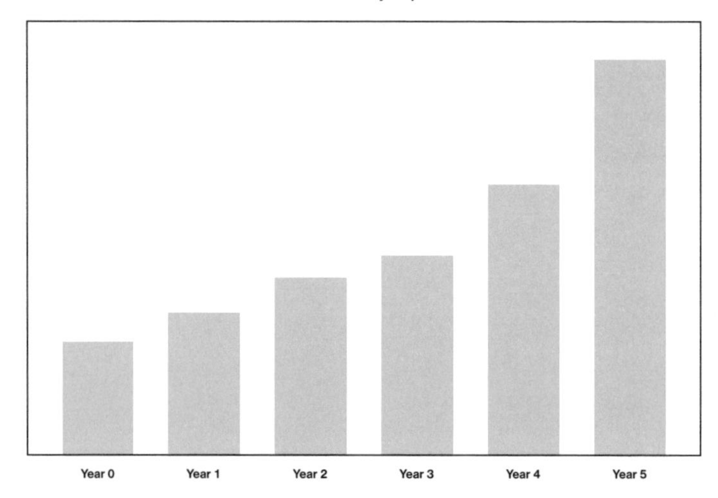

Over five years, that means the money could multiply by over three times, because the 28% per year compounds.

But in the *worst case*, that money could decrease by 11% per year (on average). That happened from 1928 to 1933.

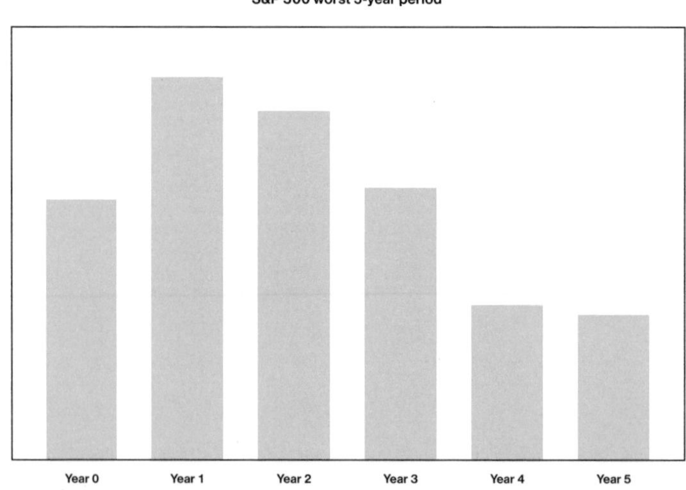

So, if you withdrew five years later, it would only have been worth about half as much.

Thus, if you invest your money in the total stock market for five years, you'll likely earn between -11% per year (*losing* 11% per year) and 28% per year—which is a big range! Over that time horizon, the total stock market does seem risky. But it's still less risky than it is over a one-year period.

When we expand the timeline from five years to twenty years (meaning, you invest the money and don't touch it until twenty years later), that range decreases further. Over twenty years, the best that the total stock market could do is grow by 17% per year on average. It did that from 1979 to 1999.

S&P 500 best 20-year period

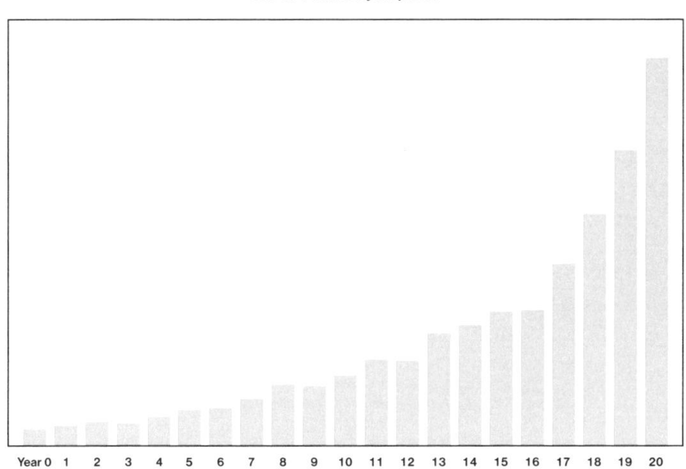

And the worst that the total stock market could do is grow by 3% per year on average. It did that from 1929 to 1949.

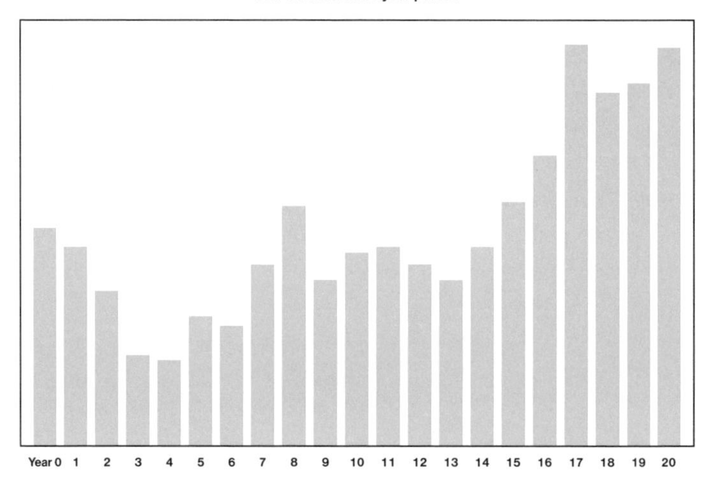

Not bad! That "worst-case" scenario is still 3% per year, which means your money would almost double after twenty years.

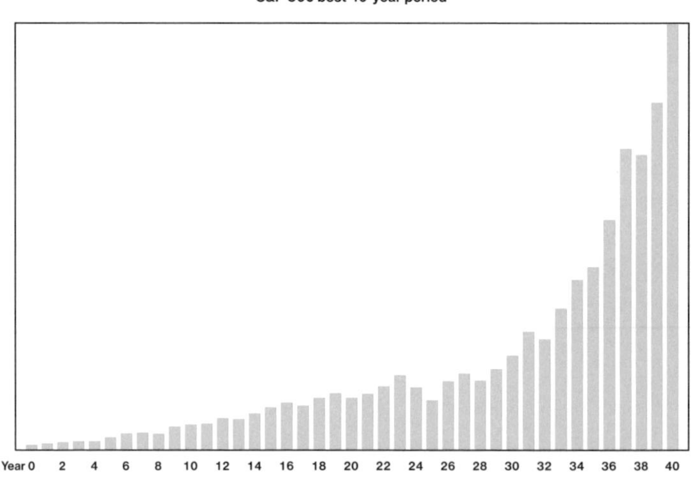

Lastly, over a forty-year period, the range is even smaller. The best is 12% per year on average. That happened from 1950 to 1990.

And the worst is 5% per year on average.[15] That happened from 1881 to 1921.

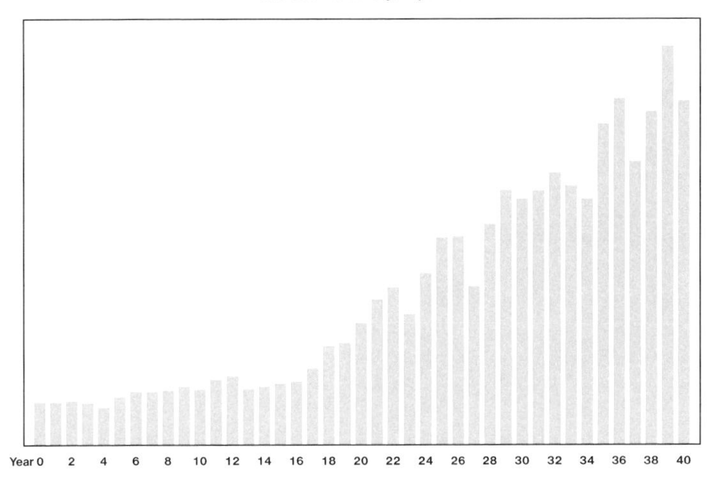

Putting it all together, this chart shows you how much risk there is in investing in the total stock market, depending on how long you're investing:

[15] By "per year on average," I mean that I'm taking the total growth over a period of time (like forty years) and averaging it to come up with the average growth each year. So "12% per year on average over forty years" is the same as "9,300% total over forty years" (if you annualize 9,300% over forty years, you get 12% per year).

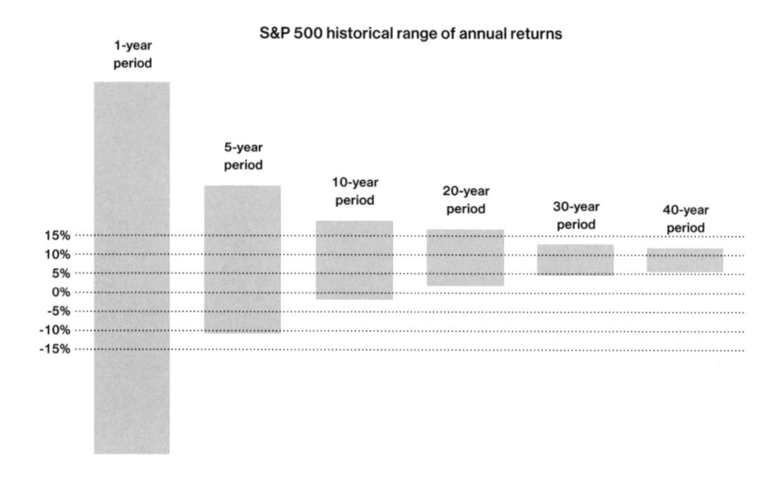

For example, if you invested over a one-year period, your returns could have ranged from negative 43% per year to positive 55% per year on average. But if you invested over a forty-year period, your returns could have ranged from positive 5% to positive 12% on average (no less).

This is the most important chart in this entire book (and perhaps in any book you will ever read). Look at it again!

In your own words, what is this chart implying?

Here are my words: The longer you keep your money invested in the total stock market, the narrower your range of possible returns. Over a thirty-year or more period, it nearly ceases to become risky.

This data so far has all been based on the historical performance of the total stock market since 1870. If we restrict it to a more modern period, like 1960 and onward, the ranges get even smaller. Over any forty-year period since 1960, the total stock market grew 8.5% per year on average in the worst case, and 12% per year on average in the best case.

That includes the "great recession" caused by the housing bubble in 2008. Even if you withdrew your money from an S&P 500 index fund during that recession, at the end of 2009, as long as you had invested it forty years earlier (at the end of 1969), it would have grown by 8.7% per year on average—it would have multiplied by twenty-eight!

Over these long time horizons, the total stock market looks different than it does day to day. It's unlikely to return much less than 9% per year on average.

So, is the total stock market volatile? Yes.

But is it risky in the long term? Probably not.

Of course, there's no guarantee that the total stock market's value will continue to increase as it has historically. The United States has been a relatively stable country, but in countries whose governments collapse or undergo radical change, the total stock market itself can evaporate. Similarly, if the United States were to move away from a purely free-market economic system, or the population growth were to significantly change, that could change our 150-year historical trajectory. Keep in mind, however, that the data since 1870 includes multiple bubbles and stock market crashes, the Great Depression of the 1930s, both World Wars, and 9/11.

I don't like the term "stock market crash" because, at least in the United States, the stock market has never truly crashed. Every time it's gone down, it's gone back up even higher than before within a few years. The term "crash" causes unnecessary panicking and foolish decision-making. Instead, many people refer to crashes as **recessions**. Recessions are a normal part of a free-market economy. They can be very painful while they're happening, but in the long term, the total stock market grows again to become better off than it was before.

All right, assuming you're convinced that investing in the total stock market is the way to go for the long term (such as retirement), *how* do you actually do that? Do you need to buy 500 stocks yourself? No! You can utilize . . .

Mutual funds

A **mutual fund** is a collection of assets (for example, stocks and bonds) that is managed by a person or company (the **fund manager**). Rather than buying those assets themselves, you can just buy shares of the mutual fund itself.

For example, an S&P 500 index fund is a mutual fund that tracks the S&P 500; it has those five hundred stocks (with amounts weighted to those company's sizes). The fund manager makes sure the weighting stays balanced, and if a company gets booted off the S&P 500 list, they sell it and purchase its replacement.

An exchange-traded fund, abbreviated **ETF**, is basically the same as a mutual fund. The only difference is that it can be bought and sold like a stock.[16] ETFs also have some tax advantages that mutual funds don't (since they are not obligated to pay distributions each year).

Mutual funds and ETFs are incredibly useful; to me, large index funds in particular are one of the wonders of the modern world! They make retirement affordable to millions of people by letting them share in the prosperity of the total stock market.

However, there are two things you must watch out for with mutual funds: fees and taxes.

16 Normally, with a mutual fund, you buy shares directly from the mutual fund company. If you want a certain ETF, you don't need to buy it from the ETF company—you can buy it on the stock market, using any stockbroker. For example, the company Vanguard manages a mutual fund called the Vanguard 500 Index Fund, which follows the S&P 500. They also have an ETF called Vanguard S&P 500 ETF. The ETF has a ticker symbol, VOO, just like a stock would.

1. Fees – Every mutual fund has an **expense ratio**, meaning how much they charge you to manage the fund. For example, if you invested $100 in a fund whose expense ratio is 1%, then every year they will take $1 of your money for themselves. If your investment grows to, say, $110, then that year they will take $1.10 of your money. The average mutual fund expense ratio is between 0.5% and 1%.[17]

2. Taxes – Every transaction a mutual fund makes (buying or selling a stock) incurs taxes. That's because most of your capital gains (increases in the value of your assets) are "unrealized," meaning they are not taxed until you actually sell the shares and "realize" (get) the profit. The more active a fund manager is in buying and selling, the more often the gains will be realized and you will get taxed.

On average, **active funds** (mutual funds that try to pick the best stocks) incur higher fees and taxes, while **passive funds** (mutual funds that track indexes, such as the S&P 500) incur lower fees and taxes.

Interestingly, even two funds that look almost identical can have wildly varying expense ratios, depending on who is managing them. There are many mutual fund companies, and each has many mutual funds, so you always need to compare their expense ratios.

If you're deciding between two nearly identical funds that have nearly the same expense ratios (for example, an S&P 500 index fund offered by Fidelity and an S&P 500 index fund offered by Vanguard that each have a 0.06 expense ratio), then I typically recommend picking the one managed by Vanguard.[18] Why? Unlike the vast majority of finance companies, Vanguard is essentially a nonprofit; the funds themselves own the company Vanguard. So, if you own

---

17 Sometimes you will see 0.5% written as "50 basis points" or 1% as "100 basis points." A **basis point** just means one-hundredth of a percent.

18 Full disclosure: I worked for a short time at Vanguard. It's an amazing company! The founder, John Bogle, pioneered the creation of large index funds that were accessible to the public. (We Bogle fans are often referred to as "Bogleheads.")

any shares of a Vanguard-run mutual fund, you also own a piece of Vanguard the company. That means their incentives are aligned with the goals of the fund holders, most of whom are ordinary investors like you, who are saving for retirement—so the fund managers are much less likely to try to pull shenanigans on you (which are all too common in the investing world).

However, even with the most passive of funds, taxes will still eat away at your growth. For example, let's say you invest $1,000 for forty years and it grows at an average of 9% per year. Without being taxed, you'd end up with $31,000. But if you had to pay 20% of your earnings each year in taxes, it would effectively be growing at 7.2% (80% of 9%), and you'd end up with only $16,000—about *half* as much.

Of course, taxes are mandatory (and we'll learn more about how to pay them in the next chapter). Fortunately, there is an incredible way to reduce the impact of taxes on your investments if you are saving them specifically for retirement . . .

Retirement accounts

You've probably heard of a 401(k) (or a 403(b) for a nonprofit or a TSP for the government). It's a type of **retirement account**: an investment that has major tax benefits as long as you don't withdraw from it before age fifty-nine and a half. A 401(k) has two tax benefits:

1. Tax-deferred distributions – Any distributions (capital gains, dividends, or interest) that you earn from the investment are taxed later, instead of now. In other words, the tax you would have to pay on your investment's growth each year gets deferred (delayed) until you withdraw from the account.

Why does that matter? Because of compounding! If you earn $10 on a $100 investment this year and have to pay $2 (20%) in taxes, then only $8, rather than the full $10, will grow over time. It's much better to pay $2 in taxes later instead of now because that $2 itself will grow exponentially.

To use our previous example of $1,000 invested for forty years at 9% growth and with a 20% tax rate: If you pay the taxes each year, you will end up with $16,000, but if you defer the taxes until you withdraw the money forty years later, you will end up with $25,000.

2. Tax-deferred income – The income you earn that goes into the retirement account also will not get taxed until you withdraw it. As you probably know, in addition to paying taxes on your investments, you also need to pay tax on your income. Paying less tax on your income today means you can invest more today, and that additional investment will compound over time.

Using the example from above, if you could afford to invest $1,000 of your post-tax money (the amount of money you actually take home), then you can afford to invest $1,250 of your pre-tax money. After forty years, you'll end up with $31,000 instead of $25,000.

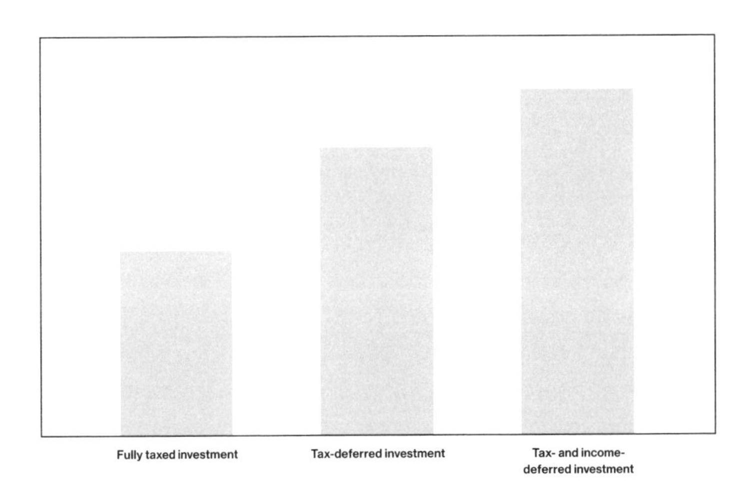

The 401(k) is a very specific type of retirement account called an **employer-sponsored** retirement account—meaning, your employer offers it to you. You can decide how much money you want to deduct (subtract) from each of your paychecks, and your employer will automatically put that amount into the account.

- Cons: Your employer decides which mutual funds you can invest the 401(k) in (sometimes, the one you want won't be available). And, there's a maximum (which is currently $23,000 per year).
- Pros: Often, your employer will offer a 401(k) "match," meaning they will give you extra cash (in addition to your regular salary). For example, if they have a $3,000 match, that means that if you contribute up to $3,000 to your 401(k), they will pay you *another* $3,000, directly into your 401(k).

We'll get into the specifics of how you should allocate your retirement savings soon. But for now, to state the obvious: It's almost always the best move to "max the match," meaning contribute to your 401(k) the full amount your employer matches. It's basically free money that your employer won't pay you unless you use the 401(k). (Another way of thinking about it: It's a 100%, risk-free rate of return on your investment.)

FAQ: Why do employers offer a match, rather than just paying you more in regular salary, which you could choose to spend or invest however you want?

I would certainly prefer that! Offering a match lets your employer take advantage of a legal loophole called "safe harbor," by which they can get around limits on executive compensation. For better or worse, offering a 401(k) match (rather than simply paying you more) has become standard in many industries.

In addition to a 401(k)—or if you don't have an employer that offers one—you can open an **individual retirement account** (IRA). Each year, you can contribute up to $7,000 into your IRA in addition to the 401(k) limit. There are two types of IRAs:

1. Traditional IRA – This one works just like a 401(k): It has tax-deferred distributions plus tax-deferred income.

2. Roth IRA – This one does not have tax-deferred income. However, it has tax-free (not tax-deferred) distributions. Meaning, you can only put post-tax money into it (money you've already paid income tax on), but—as long as you're fifty-nine and a half or older—you can withdraw money from it without paying any taxes at all.

A mnemonic to remember this difference: With a **R**oth IRA, you pay income tax **R**ight now; with a **T**raditional IRA, you pay income tax **T**omorrow.

Which one is better? It depends how much you're able to contribute:

- If you can meet the $7,000 limit – A Roth IRA is definitely better. Think of it this way: By contributing seven thousand post-tax dollars, you're "squeezing" more money into it. Contributing $7,000 into a Traditional IRAis really like contributing $5,600 (assuming a 20% tax rate), since you will eventually be taxed that 20% (when you withdraw)—which, under our typical assumptions, will be worth $175,000 in forty years. But if you can afford to pay the 20% tax now and contribute more, you can squeeze in $7,000—which will be worth $220,000 in forty years.
- If you cannot meet the $7,000 limit – It's a toss-up. You basically have to guess whether your income tax rate is going to be higher in the future than it is today. If it's the same, the benefits of the two IRAs will come out exactly

even. If it's higher in the future, Roth IRA is better, so you can take advantage of your present lower tax rate by paying those income taxes now. But it's hard to guess . . . On the one hand, hopefully your career will have an upward trajectory, so you'll be in a much higher income bracket when you're in your sixties; on the other hand, you will hopefully be retired when you start withdrawing from your IRA, so your only income will be your withdrawals (plus Social Security).

Other types of investments

So far we've been focusing on the total stock market, which you can invest in via funds like an S&P 500 index fund. That's the ideal plan for money you're saving for retirement. But what if you're investing money that you want to use in the short term for a big purchase, like a car, grad-school tuition, or a house? With that money, you do care about volatility. For example, your investment could grow like this over multiple years:

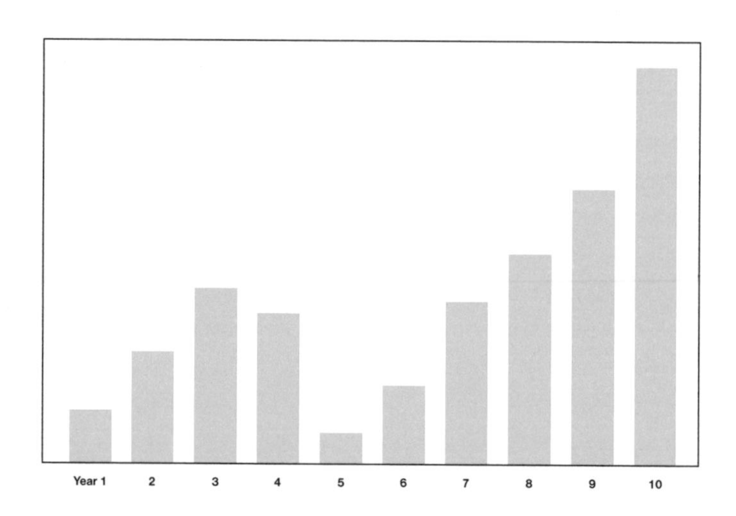

What if you have a mortgage payment due in year five? You don't care about the growth in the long term—you need it now, and you lost most of it! There are plenty of options for investments that are less volatile than the total stock market:

- For money you'll need in three to eight years – A **bond index fund** may be your best bet. Bonds earn between 1 and 5% per year on average. They are somewhat volatile and can even lose value (because bond prices can decrease when the Federal Reserve increases interest rates), but they are less volatile than stocks. And just as with stocks, the best way to diversify away the risk of individual bonds is to use an index of bonds.
- For money you'll need in six months to three years – **A certificate of deposit (CD)** from a bank is a good idea. A CD is a special type of bank account, from which you promise not to withdraw the money you put in for a certain amount of time (usually you can select six months, one year, eighteen months, or two years). In exchange, the bank offers you a higher interest rate than a typical savings account—usually these range between 1 to 4%. This interest is guaranteed, so there's no volatility involved. A **high-yield savings account** is similar (it offers a higher interest rate than a typical bank account), and sometimes has fewer restrictions than a CD.
- For money you'll need in the next six months – Keep it in cash. If you need the money at any point in the near future, you don't want to risk not being able to withdraw it from a CD.

Your investing plan

There is a lot more you could learn about investing. But as of now, you know all the fundamentals you need in order to put together a basic financial plan that will protect you in both the short and the long term.

Here is what I typically recommend to the average person in their twenties:

1. Insurance – Get enough insurance to prevent nightmare scenarios from ruining your life, namely automotive liability insurance and basic health insurance (we'll cover this in a lot more detail in skill #7). You don't want one accident to destroy your financial future.

2. Pay off high-interest debt – Any debt with interest rates higher than 10%, namely credit card debt, is "expensive" (it grows faster than your investments in the total stock market, which typically average 9% per year).

3. Build an emergency fund – Save up enough cash, in a bank account, to cover your expenses for three to six months, in case you lose your job or have an urgent large expense.

4. Max the match on your 401(k) – However much your employer matches, put that much into your 401(k).[19] It's basically free additional salary that you're leaving on the table if you don't. Pick whichever fund your employer offers that tracks the total stock market index or the S&P 500 index and has the lowest expense ratio (fees).

19 Note: If you no longer work for this employer, you will be able to roll over (convert) your 401(k) into an IRA. So, it will continue to grow tax-free and you will have more control over which funds it can be invested in.

5. Max your IRA– If you can invest up to the current $7,000 limit, pick a Roth IRA instead of a Traditional IRA. You can open a retirement account online with a mutual fund company (as you know, I like Vanguard) and select their version of an S&P 500 index fund (in Vanguard's case, the one labeled VFIAX).

6. Pay off lower-interest debt – For example, student debt or a car loan in the range of 5 to 10%. Paying off that debt is essentially investing with guaranteed growth of 5 to 10% (since that's what they'd be charging you if you don't pay it off).

7. Short-term investments – If you're saving up for a large purchase, refer to the bullet points above regarding which investments to pick based on the time sensitivity of your purchase. For example, if you know you *must* pay your grad-school tuition in one year, pick an option that is less volatile. But if you know you want to buy a house any time in the next five to ten years, pick an option with a higher potential rate of return—because if there's a recession, you're willing to just wait it out until your investment regrows before making the purchase.

The most common investing mistakes

Kelly and Shellie both invested $6,500 each year in a Roth IRA, in an S&P 500 index fund. After twenty years, at the age of forty-five, their investments are now worth $410,000—the stock market has grown, on average, at 10% per year.

Then the market crashes. Kelly's and Shellie's retirement savings are now worth only $278,000. Kelly panics. She says, "My investments are no longer safe! I lost almost one-third of my savings in the blink of an eye. Maybe an S&P 500 index fund worked for my parents' generation, but not for mine." She switches all the money in her IRA into a low-risk bond fund that grows consistently by 1% per year.

Shellie says, "The total stock market fluctuates all the time. It's had really bad years a few times in the past. But really good years also happen, and they average out the really bad years—that's why the average is 9% per year in the long run." She decides to keep her investments as is.

What happens over the next twenty years? When Kelly and Shellie retire in 2063, Kelly now has $470,000 and Shellie has $2,000,000. If Kelly hopes to live for another thirty years, then accounting for inflation, she only has $4,800 to spend each year—not enough to get by.

It turns out, the numbers in this story weren't made up! For the hypothetical years 2023 through 2063, I used the exact same numbers as the total stock market from 1953 to 1993. (In 1974, it really did lose over 20%, and over the following years, it really did recover. Over that forty-year period, it averaged more than 10% growth per year.)

The lesson is clear: Don't panic!

When a downturn happens, some people think, "I lost one-third of my savings!" Of course, they would only be losing money if they withdrew from their investments during the recession. Despite this logic, many people do exactly the opposite. That kind of panicking and withdrawing actually makes recessions worse for everyone else, because people lose confidence in the economy and it becomes harder for businesses to borrow or raise money.

Once you've invested your money, don't check up on it every day. You can look at it every so often for planning or budgeting purposes, but obsessing over your long-term investments can only lead to panicking, or to . . .

The second investing pitfall: overconfidence.

As an exercise, let's say your friend wants to keep her investments in an active fund. She says, "After one year with this active fund, I've earned 10% returns, whereas the total stock market earned 9% that year. Clearly I picked the best fund manager."

What would you tell your friend?

Here's my answer: That's results-oriented thinking. Just because your fund manager pick happened to turn out well this year doesn't make it the right decision. On average, trading stocks won't beat the total stock market. And because of the fees, you lose money on average. In fact, if the fee you paid is over 1% (as is often the case), you might have even lost money this year, when compared to the alternative of investing in an S&P 500 index fund. It's like saying, "I survived a shark attack, therefore sharks are harmless."

An average of 9% per year in the long term is a great goal—but it will not make you rich. Sure, winning at the slot machines (or trading individual stocks) can make you rich, but it can just as likely make you poor. To paraphrase Burton Malkiel, an acclaimed investor: "There's no such thing as getting rich quickly. Only getting poor quickly."

If you're still interested in more speculative investing, like trading stocks, there's nothing wrong with that, as long as your expectations are low. If you love tracking Apple's performance and want some stake in that game, go ahead—just not with the savings that you need. As with playing the slot machines, it may be completely worth it because of the pleasure you get out of it. If you beat the growth of the S&P 500, cool! If not, you should still have enough in other investments to afford retirement.

The final pitfall may be the opposite of what you're expecting to hear: Don't care *too much* about your investing. Optimizing your rate of return is important—but not as important as your salary. Even one raise of $2,000 that lasts throughout your career is as good as getting an additional, consistent one-percentage-point higher growth in all of your investments (something fund managers would kill for). Later (in skills #12 & #13) we'll discuss how to optimize your career.

SUMMARY

- Unless you invest, you will probably not have enough money to live on during retirement (especially accounting for inflation).
- Compounding is when the money that you earn in turn earns you more money.
- An S&P 500 index fund (which tracks the five hundred largest companies, and mirrors the growth of the total US stock market) earns 9% on average in the long term.
- Almost no one can beat the total stock market's growth consistently; past performance for stock traders and fund managers is no indication of future performance (claiming otherwise would be results-oriented thinking).
- In the short term, the total stock market is volatile; but in the long term, the range of possible returns is very narrow (between 5 to 12% per year on average).
- For most people, the best way to invest for retirement is to use a Roth IRA invested in a passive fund, such as an S&P 500 index fund.
- Be careful not to fall prey to panicking (so, for retirement investments, stay the course), overconfidence (so only gamble with money you can afford to lose), or focusing on investing at the expense of your career (which is much more important).

Homework

For your 401(k), if your employer currently offers one, check:

- Where is it currently invested? If you can, switch it into a low-cost stock index fund.
- How much does your employer match? How much are you contributing? If you can afford to, deduct more from each paycheck to maximize the match.

If you need any help answering these questions or taking these steps, contact your company's human resources department, who are usually happy to help.

Then, set up an IRA:

- Create an online account with a mutual fund (such as Vanguard).
- Open an IRA (probably a Roth IRA).
- Connect your bank account and transfer money into it.
- Choose where to invest the money (probably in their version of an S&P 500 index fund, such as VFIAX).

Make sure you have enabled the option for "reinvestment"—this is critical! Usually it's a little box that is checked off by default, but not always. This means that any capital gains, dividends, and interest earned by the funds will go back into the fund—to compound over time—rather than being paid out to you now in cash.

Extra credit: Open a CD or high-yield savings account with your bank so you can earn a higher interest rate on any cash that you're sure you won't need to spend in the next six months.

Skill #7

GET INSURANCE AND PAY TAXES

I'm sensing some hesitancy. You may have had to take a deep breath before turning to this page. You might have thought, "I just finished the second least fun topic in this whole book, and how am I rewarded? Now I need to get through the least fun one—and wait, it's actually two least fun topics at once."

It's true, the investing chapter was quite technical. The topics in this chapter do require a similar level of detail in order to understand them—and perhaps the takeaways will have less of a "wow" factor than what you learned about investing. However, knowing about insurance and taxes is *even more important* than knowing about investing.

That's because they are the two financial commitments that are necessary. In many states, you are required to have health insurance and car insurance; in all states, you are required to pay your taxes. If you don't, you can be fined thousands of dollars, and can even be imprisoned. (All the more reason I find it so crazy that they don't teach these things in school!)

In addition to avoiding government penalties, there's plenty of upside to understanding these topics; it can save you thousands of dollars per year.

So, are you ready?

Of course you are! You're doing great. And once you get through the rest of this chapter, you'll find that the rest of the book is much less technical. (You might even miss this chapter, and all of the shenanigans and bad jokes I added to it to make it extra fun.)

And if you're still mad at me for being sneaky by squeezing together two dry topics into one chapter, what can I say . . . it's still not nearly as sneaky as some tricks employed by the US tax code or by insurance salespeople!

How insurance works

Insurance is when you pay a company on a regular basis so that they'll pay *you* if something specific happens. For example, with car insurance, you pay a bill every month. If you get into a car accident, the insurance company will pay you enough to cover (part of) the costs.

The point is: You're willing to pay in order to make the possible event of a disaster slightly less disastrous for you.

The contract between you and the insurance company is called the **policy**. The bill you pay each month is the **premium**. When an event happens that is "covered by" (included in) the policy, you submit a **claim** to the insurance company, and they reimburse you with a **payout** equal to the damage caused, up to the dollar **limit** specified in your policy.

For example, if you got into a car accident, you'd see that your insurance policy covers damage to your car. It also probably covers **liability**, which is what you owe someone else if you caused the accident (or if they sue you). You'd submit a claim describing these things, and the insurance company would reimburse you with a payout.

However, the payout usually isn't the full amount of the claim you request—it's reduced by a **deductible**. In other words, the deductible is the amount of the disaster that you have to pay from your own pocket. For damage to your car, the deductible might be $500—so you would pay for the first $500 in repairs, and the insurance company would pay the rest.

In general, policies with higher deductibles cost you less (in premiums). If you're willing to cover more of the cost of a disaster yourself, the insurance's payout will be smaller; therefore, they're willing to charge you less for the insurance.

Certain types of insurance often protect you against multiple things. For example, homeowners' insurance not only covers damage to your property, it also covers liability for others being hurt on your property (if they trip on your doorstep and sue you). And to make it more complicated, there are almost infinite different types of insurance. Doctors buy malpractice insurance (to cover them if they're sued by a patient); newspapers buy libel insurance (to cover them if they're sued for defaming someone); media companies can even buy celebrity insurance (to cover them in case their star gets caught up in a scandal).

How insurance companies work

You might be familiar with the names of the largest insurance companies: Berkshire Hathaway, Allianz, MetLife, AIG. Many insurance companies also specialize in one area; for example, Geico and Progressive are companies that mostly sell car insurance.

Insurance companies collect the regular payments from premiums. Most people, of course, never suffer from a major disaster—and that's why insurance companies have a lot of cash in reserve. And what's the best thing to do with lots of money that probably won't need to be spent for a while? Invest it! Insurance companies are some of the largest investors in the world.

Insurance salespeople are known as **agents**. They can be "captive agents," meaning they are employed by an insurance company to sell that company's policies exclusively. Alternatively, they can be "independent agents," who work for an insurance agency. An insurance *agency* is not an insurance *company*—an agency sells policies that are supplied by insurance companies, often helping customers shop around from multiple insurance companies. Nowadays, many agencies, such as Policygenius, function like online marketplaces where you can shop for insurance policies (comparing prices and coverage).

Insurance companies want to know your risk level, meaning the chances that a disaster will occur and they'll have to pay. They employ **underwriters** to price their policies. Sometimes, underwriters work at an individual level, investigating customers who want a new policy. Other times, they set general rules. For example, a smoker is more likely to die younger, so life insurance is more expensive for them; someone above the age of twenty-five is more likely to have more experience behind the wheel, so car insurance is cheaper for them.

Of course, selling insurance is only worth it for the company if what you pay in premiums outweighs the risk you pose. The underwriters use statistics and probabilities to make sure that, on average, the company comes out ahead.

So if it's always a good deal for the insurance company, why would you want to buy insurance? There's one important difference between you and an insurance company: If a disaster occurs, to an insurance company that's just some money they lose—but to you, it's *your life* that may be ruined. So, it's worth it for you to make sure your (unlikely) disasters are less disastrous to you.

That's why I actually think insurance is an amazing invention! It benefits both sides—insurance companies like making a profit, and I like being able to drive without worrying about the fact that if I accidentally hit someone they could sue me for millions of dollars.

We'll go over the five most important types of insurance you can buy, with an eye toward these questions:

- What does it cover?
- How much does it cost?
- Is it worth getting?

Car insurance

What does it cover?

There are multiple components of car insurance coverage:

If an accident is your fault:

Damage to others and their property:

1. Bodily Injury – Covers the other driver's (and their passengers') medical bills.
2. Property Damage – Covers the repair or replacement of the other driver's car, or other property (if, for example, you crash into a building).

Damage to yourself / your property:

3. Personal Injury – Covers your medical bills (and also sometimes lost income in case you're unable to work).
4. Collision – Covers the repair or replacement of your car.

If an accident is not your fault:

5. Comprehensive – Covers your car being stolen, hit while parked (by an unknown driver), hitting an animal, or being damaged by fire, flood, or storm.
6. Underinsured Motorists – Covers your medical bills and car damage if the accident is someone else's fault, but they do not have insurance coverage to pay for all of it.
7. Uninsured Motorists – Covers your medical bills and car damage if the accident is someone else's fault, but they do not have insurance at all.

Wait, why do you need #6 and #7? Isn't every driver required by law to get car insurance? Yes, in nearly all states, car insurance is mandatory for all drivers. However, some people simply ignore that law: 14% of drivers in the United States are uninsured. It's also possible that the other person does have insurance, but the limit on their payout is lower than your bills. For example, if their bodily injury limit is $25,000 but your medical bills are $40,000, then your underinsured motorist insurance would cover the $15,000 difference. Hence, underinsured motorists insurance is *critical.* The majority of drivers don't have enough insurance (a high enough liability limit) to cover your expenses if they hit you!

Here's a handy chart that summarizes all seven types of coverage that car insurance typically includes:

FAULT STATES	Accident: your fault (including hitting stationary objects)	Accident: their fault	Other: theft, hit while parked, hit an animal, fire/flood/storm
Their (and their passengers') medical expenses	Your Bodily Injury (liability)	Their Personal Injury	
Their property damage	Your Property Damage (liability)	Their Collision	
Your (and your passengers') medical expenses	Your Personal Injury	Their Bodily Injury (liability) OR Your Uninsured/Underinsured Motorists (if they are uninsured/underinsured)	
Your property damage	Your Collision	Their Property Damage (liability) OR Your Collision (if they are uninsured/underinsured)	Your Comprehensive

There's one exception to some of these rules, called **no-fault states**: states where the person who caused an accident is *not* liable (responsible) for the other person's medical expenses.

FAQ: How do no-fault states work?

Welcome to the no-fault sidebar! If you don't want to read all of this, that really isn't your fault. If you do . . .

Note that no-fault states have limits. If your medical expenses are higher than a certain cutoff, you can sue the other person to get them to pay the bill. That's why most no-fault states still require bodily injury (liability) insurance. In fact, the no-fault rule ends up not mattering in many cases—insurance companies of each party will work things out (including settling lawsuits) behind the scenes based on who they think is at fault.

The no-fault states are Florida, Hawaii, Kansas, Kentucky, Massachusetts, Michigan, Minnesota, New Jersey, New York, North Dakota, Pennsylvania, and Utah, plus Puerto Rico and Washington, DC.

NO-FAULT STATES	Accident: your fault (including hitting stationary objects)	Accident: their fault	Other: theft, hit while parked, hit an animal, fire/flood/storm
Their (and their passengers') medical expenses	Their Personal Injury, up to lawsuit cutoff—after that, your Bodily Injury (liability)	Their Personal Injury	
Their property damage	Your Property Damage (liability)	Their Collision	
Your (and your passengers') medical expenses	Your Personal Injury	Your Personal Injury, up to lawsuit cutoff—after that, their Bodily Injury (liability) OR Your Uninsured/Underinsured Motorists (if they are uninsured/underinsured)	
Your property damage	Your Collision	Their Property Damage (liability) OR Your Collision (if they are uninsured/underinsured)	Your Comprehensive

Many car insurance policies cover both *you* and any car you borrow, as well as *your car* and anyone who borrows it. However, it can vary, so it's definitely worth checking your policy before you lend your car to someone or borrow theirs.

One annoying thing about car insurance: Filing a claim typically increases your premium. In other words, if you get into an accident, you will have to pay more for your insurance in the future. That's because knowing you were in an accident makes the insurance company assume you're a worse driver than they previously thought.

If you need to repair your car, and the cost is lower than the deductible you have to pay for collision (if it was an accident) or comprehensive (if it was something else), there's no reason to file an insurance claim. You'll still have to pay the same amount to get your car fixed, plus the insurance company might raise your premium. I learned about this the hard way.[20]

How much does it cost?

It varies by state, and it depends on your risk factors, such as your age and driving history. It also depends on how much coverage you want.

The average cost of car insurance in the United States is $2,100/year. (Owning a car is expensive! You have to pay that insurance premium, plus gas, parking, maintenance, and repairs, not to mention the cost of the car itself.)

As an example, here is the current car insurance policy I have from Geico, which covers my wife and me, for the two cars we own:

---

20 Once, my car's windshield had a small crack. Apparently you can fix that pretty easily at little cost, but I didn't know that. I was an hour away from home, driving in New Jersey. Suddenly, I heard the loudest BANG of my life! The crack had tripled in size. I pulled over frantically—by pure luck that happened to be at a rest stop, where someone helped me out. In the end, the cost of repairing the windshield was about $300, which was below our $500 comprehensive deductible, so I had to pay for the whole thing myself. On the bright side, our premium did not go up.

1. Bodily Injury: $250,000/$500,000
2. Property Damage: $100,000
3. Personal Injury: $100,000
4. Collision: $500 deductible
5. Comprehensive: $500 deductible
6. Underinsured Motorist: $250,000/$500,000
7. Uninsured Motorist: $250,000/$500,000 (bodily injury), $100,000 (property damage)

Premium: $2,319/year

Note that the slashes indicate "per person / per accident." Essentially, the number after the slash is the maximum. For example, if I caused an accident and the other person sued me for their medical bills (bodily injury), the insurance would cover up to $250,000 per person I injured. But if multiple people were injured, my policy would cover at most $500,000 for the accident.

Is it worth getting?

Well, if you drive then you don't really have a choice. Some form of car insurance is required in all states (except Virginia and New Hampshire). The requirements include minimum amounts on the limits. For example, California requires that you buy a policy with a bodily injury limit of at least $15,000/$30,000.

Regardless of your state's requirements, I strongly recommend that you cover yourself in every situation, which means you need some amount of each type in your policy.

The most important coverage, by far, is liability—you don't want to go bankrupt if someone sues you over an accident. I'd recommend purchasing *at least* bodily injury of $100,000 per person / $300,000 per accident, and property damage of $100,000 per accident.

Even with great insurance, car accidents are still a major hassle. You have to file an insurance claim, get the repairs, and so on. Not to mention that money may be the least of your worries if you're seriously injured. Nothing can guarantee you'll never have an accident, but driving safely can greatly reduce the risk!

FAQ: Do I always need collision and comprehensive coverage? Not necessarily, if you have an old car. Remember, you have to pay the entire deductible—so if your deductible is $1,000 and you could replace your car by purchasing a used car for the same amount of money, there's no point in paying a premium each year. (Alternatively, you might want to pay a *higher* premium to get a lower deductible—sometimes this can be pretty cheap for comprehensive.)

Property insurance

What does it cover?

If you own a home, then **homeowners' insurance** covers your property, such as furniture and clothing, the physical dwelling, and liability (for example, if someone sues you after tripping on your garden hose).

If you rent, **renters' insurance** covers only your property—the structure and the liability are your landlord's responsibility.

How much does it cost?

The average cost of homeowners' insurance in the United States is about $1,400/year. It depends, of course, upon the location (for example, is it a high-crime area?) and the structure (for example, is it an old building?).

Renters' insurance costs an average of $150/year. The more coverage you want, the more it costs. For example, covering $5,000 of your personal belongings will incur lower premiums than covering $10,000 of your personal belongings.

Is it worth getting?

Many lenders (mortgage providers) require that you get homeowners' insurance.

However, if you are just renting, renters' insurance often goes overlooked—45% of renters don't have it at all. The question to ask yourself is: If a disaster occurred and I lost everything in my apartment, would I have the means to financially recover? If the answer is yes—if you could rely on your paycheck, or your parents, to build you back up—it may not be necessary. If the answer is no, it may be worth getting ASAP.

Ironic story: Years ago, I created an app to teach people personal finance, including much of this lesson about insurance. The software engineer who was coding the Android app was living at his girlfriend's place. While they were out one day, her home was burgled, and all of their valuables were stolen. She didn't have renters' insurance. He no longer had his laptop and phone, which made it impossible for him to keep working for a while (and during that lost time, think about how many more people were not learning that they, too, should be getting renters' insurance!).

If you do get it, it's probably worth paying for an amount of coverage equal to what you estimate your property is worth. For example, if all your clothing, electronics, furniture, cookware, jewelry, and other belongings adds up to $10,000, you'll want to pay for a policy that has $10,000 of coverage.

When you obtain a renters' insurance policy, take fifteen minutes to go through your apartment and film everything you own. That way, if you ever do need to file a claim, you'll remember what you lost—and have proof that you owned it.

Life insurance

What does it cover?

When you die,[21] **life insurance** pays money to the people who outlive you. You designate these **beneficiaries** in advance. For example, if you have a $1,000,000 life insurance policy, then when you die, your beneficiaries will get the payout of $1,000,000.

The regular version is called **term life insurance**. For some set amount of time, such as twenty years, you pay a monthly premium that remains the same. The term helps you lock in a rate for a certain number of years, since when you get older your risk factors will be higher and life insurance will be much more expensive—because you are more likely to die (sorry!), they will charge you more.

There's another type called **whole life insurance** (or **cash value life insurance**), which is more complicated. Essentially, a portion of your premium goes into a savings account that gets invested for you. Because of a random tax law, the investment grows tax-deferred, and the withdrawal is tax-free if your heirs withdraw it after you die. However, the premiums on cash value policies are usually much higher because they give a greater piece of the pie (a commission) to the insurance agent who sells you the policy. Sometimes the agent makes as much as one and a half times what you pay in the first year as a commission! After that, they often take 5 to 8% per year. Would you invest in a mutual fund with a 5% expense ratio? I hope not! It makes a lot more sense to buy a term life insurance policy, and just invest what you can in tax-deferred retirement accounts, like an IRA. The exception is if you already have enough money to max out your IRA and 401(k) and are looking for additional ways to invest tax-free.

21 I originally wrote "If you die," but my wife, who is a hospice doctor, correctly edited this to "When you die."

How much does it cost?

Life insurance can be cheap when you're young but increase in price each year as you get older. The average cost of a twenty-year term (regular) policy for a thirty-year-old is about $200 per year, and for a sixty-year-old it's about $2,000 per year. The premium is two to three times as much if you smoke.

As with health insurance, you can usually buy life insurance through your employer. However, this isn't always the best idea, for two reasons. First, some employers charge the same premium regardless of your age (so you'll have to pay as much as someone who is older). Second, it can be difficult or expensive to transfer your policy if you switch jobs.

If you buy life insurance independently (not through your employer), you'll often be given a long questionnaire about your life activities. They may also give you a medical exam.[22] The underwriter will take all this into account to determine your premium.

Is it worth getting?

If you have a spouse or children who depend on your income, and if other family members could not fully support them if you died, then life insurance is necessary to protect them. In my case, I calculated how much money my wife would need in order to support our kids for up to twenty years, picked that coverage amount, and shopped for the cheapest policy via the website Policygenius.

If you do not have dependents, then life insurance is pretty much useless. (Sales agents will remind you that it can cover your funeral costs, but hopefully you have family members who could do that if they had to.) Keep this in mind when you are chatted up by a life insurance agent. Randomly, this super-specific type of insurance became an entire industry—with agents who are notoriously pushy.

22 In my case, this meant a very sketchy "nurse" came to my house to take my vitals and draw a blood sample. I can get queasy with needles, but I steeled myself by remembering that I could not pass out now—I needed to survive at least until the policy went into effect so my wife could get the payout!

However, you are not too young to be thinking about your will! Each state has its own laws about who gets what in the event of your death—the only way to make sure it happens the way you want is to write your wishes explicitly in a will. If your financial situation is relatively straightforward, you can use a free tool like doyourownwill.com or willing.com to help you do it in less than half an hour. Similarly, you can prepare your advance health-care directive (designate who can make your health-care decisions if you are incapacitated) and Power of Attorney (who can make your financial decisions). Just remember to keep updating these documents as you get older.

I know all of this may sound morbid. Nobody likes to think about their own death. The good thing about life insurance and wills is that you can get it done so that you don't have to worry about dying! At least, not as much.

Okay, if that didn't help lighten the mood, perhaps the next topic will: getting injured and becoming permanently disabled . . .

Disability insurance

What does it cover?

If you buy **disability insurance**, then if you become unable to work for a period of time, the insurance company will pay you a portion of your income. It doesn't pay the medical bills (that's health insurance)—only a percentage of the salary you won't be able to keep earning.

FAQ: Is this the same as workers' comp insurance?

No. Workers' compensation insurance is insurance that your employer buys from the state government. If you are injured *on the job*, then you receive compensation (income) from your employer for as long as you can't work—in exchange for you agreeing not to sue them.

The United States Social Security program does help people who are unable to work because of long-term disabilities. However, for many people, this amount (currently $1,100 per month maximum) isn't enough to cover their full cost of living.

How much does it cost?

The price depends on how much coverage you want. You could have a policy that pays you only 50% of your usual salary if you can't work, or you could have one that pays you 100%. Getting 60 to 70% coverage is typical, and the premium is somewhere between 1 to 3% of your salary. As with life insurance, the cost also depends on your age and health. If you are relatively healthy (and don't have dangerous hobbies), the premiums are lower, because you are less likely to be severely injured.

Many employers offer disability insurance, and unlike life insurance, it can be a great deal because they often subsidize part of the cost for you. Before purchasing disability insurance outside of work, check your available benefits with your human resources department first.

Is it worth getting?

For most people, 1 to 3% of income can be a lot to pay for something they may not need. So, as with life insurance, if you have a spouse, then the question is: Could they afford to live, and support you (and your children, if you have any), if you were unable to work? For many people, the answer is yes. But if not, disability insurance is necessary to protect your family against a nightmare scenario.

If you don't have a spouse, the question is: Are there people that you could depend on to support you if you were unable to work? For example, maybe your parents or other family members would be able to take care of you financially. If not, then could you afford to live on the disability income provided by Social Security? If the answer is no to that as well, then disability insurance is necessary to protect yourself.

How to buy insurance

When choosing a company to use for any type of insurance, keep in mind that you want to know not only about their policy's coverage and the premiums, but also about claims. In the worst case, an insurance company could have amazingly low premiums then simply refuse to pay out when people file claims. Talking to people and reading consumer reviews should help you avoid the outright scammers.

When you're ready, I recommend speaking to an agent (someone who sells insurance) at least once on the phone so you can ask all your questions. Don't be shy! If anything is unclear about the policy, better to ask now than be caught in a bind in the future.

Some tips on getting lower rates:

- Consolidate – If you buy multiple types of insurance (especially car insurance and renters' insurance) from the same company, they'll usually give a discount. They might also offer a discount if you have family members who use them.
- Lower your premiums by raising your deductibles – Insurance exists to prevent disasters from ruining your life. If you have enough savings to cover certain disasters (like replacing a wrecked car), you can make do with a higher deductible.
- Play hardball – Sometimes agents can lower your rates (especially if you're thinking of switching providers), but sometimes they don't have the power to do that. The good news is, even if you're not a good negotiator, you can . . .
- Just ask – Seriously. Say, "Can I please have a discount?" For example, with car insurance, you can ask if they have a safe-driver discount or a low-mileage discount. Often, a good agent will help you get lower premiums. Offer any information that has even a remote chance of being

helpful: your good driving record, your good health, your marital status, the security systems you have in your home or apartment, and so on.

You may have noticed that we haven't yet discussed the most important type of insurance yet. That's because it's so special (*cough* needlessly complicated), it gets a section of its own . . .

Health insurance

The crazy thing about health insurance in the United States is that it's really two different products wrapped into one:

1. Actual health insurance – A policy that pays out in the event of a disaster (massive medical bills that you are unlikely to be able to pay yourself).

2. A health-services subscription fee – Essentially like Netflix, but for doctors and medications. You pay to get access to a large (but limited) assortment of free or subsidized health-care services.

You can think of #1 like car insurance. You pay so that in the event of an absolute disaster—such as hitting someone with your car and being sued for everything you're worth (or, in this case, ending up in the hospital and racking up a six-figure bill)—you will be protected.

To understand #2, imagine that your car insurance covered all the basic maintenance and repairs on your car. Any time you needed an oil change, or to get the tires rotated, or even a new coat of paint, you would pay almost nothing. But, you would have to look up which auto-body shops were "in network" with your insurance plan because if you accidentally went to the wrong one they could charge you two to ten times what the actual cost of an oil change is. And, the mechanics would have no idea how much these services cost; they would perform them on your car without telling you the price, then their shop's manager would bill your insurance company.

Well, that's how health insurance works: as a subscription service, that you pay in advance, to cover the cost of your health care. However, not all of your health care is actually covered . . .

What does it cover?

Health insurance typically pays for:

- Outpatient services (like doctor's appointments or urgent-care visits)
- Inpatient services (like hospital stays or surgery)
- Medical tests (like blood draws or X-rays)
- Prescription medication

The old health insurance plans (that your parents and grandparents probably had) let you see any doctor, anywhere. Nowadays, insurance companies manage to pay less for the health care you receive because they negotiate the prices with doctors and hospitals. However, they don't have the time to negotiate with everyone, so they create a **provider network** of the providers they cover ("provider" means someone who "provides" health care, like a doctor or hospital). There are multiple ways a provider network can function, and each has its own lovely three-letter acronym.

If your insurance plan is an HMO (Health Maintenance Organization), then the policy will only pay for providers in the network. In addition, if you want to see a specialist, such as a dermatologist (skin doctor) or cardiologist (heart doctor), you need a referral from your primary-care doctor.[23]

[23] Additional clarification for the medically uninitiated: Your primary-care doctor is a general practice or family doctor that you typically see once per year for your annual checkup. A "referral" means that they send you to see the specialist because there's a medical need for it (and they tell the insurance company about that need).

By contrast, a PPO (Preferred Provider Organization) health insurance policy lets you see providers outside their network, but you do have to pay a larger share of the cost (they're more expensive than the "preferred" ones). You also get more flexibility because you don't need a referral to see a specialist. Don't worry, there's more . . . POS and EPO plans are variations on the above. This chart summarizes the differences:

	HMO	PPO	POS	EPO
Can you use an out-of-network provider?	No	Yes (but you have to pay a larger share of the cost)	Yes (but you have to pay a larger share of the cost)	No
Do you need a referral from your primary care doctor in order to see a specialist?	Yes	No	Yes	No

However, even for providers that are in-network, insurance doesn't often cover the full cost. Because, like other forms of insurance, there's a deductible you need to pay. However, instead of paying a deductible on each claim (like for each car accident), the health insurance deductible is the amount you pay each *year* before the insurance kicks in.

For example, let's say your deductible is $1,000 per year. You have to pay the full cost of all your medical expenses (other than your annual checkup), until you've spent $1,000 in the same calendar year. *After* you've spent that $1,000, the insurance will pay for the rest of the medical expenses that are covered under the policy.

Actually, I lied. The insurance won't pay for *all* covered care. There's still a portion of the costs that you have to pay: copay. If your **copay** is $50 for specialist visits, then after you've reached the deductible, if you see an in-network specialist (like a dermatologist or cardiologist), you'll pay $50, and the insurance company will pay the rest. **Coinsurance** is similar, but instead of a fixed amount, it's a percentage. Some insurance plans have coinsurance of 30% for emergency room visits. That means, after you've met the deductible, if you go to the emergency room, you'll pay 30% of the cost, and the insurance company will pay the rest.

You won't have to pay the copays and coinsurances forever, though. Most plans have an **out-of-pocket limit**, like $3,000—once you've spent that amount in one year (on the deductible and copays/coinsurances total), you won't have to pay any more copays.

In our example, let's say you've already spent $1,000 in one year, so you've met your deductible. Then, after an expensive emergency room visit, your 30% coinsurance means you end up paying $2,000. Now, you've reached the $3,000 out-of-pocket limit, so you won't have to pay any copay or coinsurance for the rest of the year.

Oh no, I lied again! Once you've reached the out-of-pocket limit, the insurance company won't pay for all covered care *forever*. You have a **maximum lifetime benefit**, which is the maximum amount the insurance company will pay for your medical costs total over the course of your entire life. Usually the maximum lifetime benefit is $1 to $2 million. (When selecting a health-care plan, there's typically no reason to worry about the maximum lifetime benefit as long as it's $1 million or higher.)

This chart summarizes everything:

As long as you're paying for your premium each month, then this happens:

NON-COVERED CARE (like an out-of-network doctor, if you have an HMO)	PREVENTATIVE CARE (like an annual checkup)	ALL OTHER COVERED CARE (like specialist visits, emergency room visits, or medical tests)
You pay the full cost	You pay nothing (or sometimes $10)	**You pay the full cost** *Until you've met the annual deductible.* Then: **You pay the copay or coinsurance** *Until you've met the annual out-of-pocket limit.* Then: **You pay nothing** *Until you've reached the maximum lifetime benefit.* Then: **You pay the full cost**

Of course, even this chart is a simplification, since there are further variations between different plans. But it gives you the basic picture.[24]

How much does it cost?

Health insurance costs a bit less than you may think because the premiums are typically tax-deductible, meaning you don't pay tax on the income that goes toward your health insurance premiums (you pay them from your salary *before* taxes are taken).

There are four main ways Americans can get health insurance:

1. Through an employer – Your employer works with a health insurance company to offer a selection of plans to employees. When you join the company, and every year thereafter, you can (re-)select which option you want, and for how many family members you would like coverage. Typically, employees do not pay the full cost of the plan because the employer subsidizes it.[25]

Typically, the cost of this plan will be the same for every employee, regardless of your "risk factors." So even if, according to an underwriter, you would be likely to cost the insurance company more money (because you'll need to make more use of health-care services), you pay the same as everyone else.

2. Through a parent – If your parent gets health insurance through their employer, and they opt for a family plan, you can remain covered until age twenty-six. (Different families have varying norms around financial independence. We'll get much deeper into this in skill #11. For now, it's worth noting this point, since many people *claim* they are financially independent yet still use their parents' health insurance.)

---

24 If you bring a picture of this flowchart to your next doctor's appointment, I will be so proud of you.

25 I remember paying about $4,000/year for health insurance at my first job. When I stopped working there, I was given the option to continue my health insurance (under a law called "COBRA")—except I would have to pay the full cost of the insurance, which was over $16,000 a year!

3. Through the government – If you don't have an employer, you can get health insurance from the "marketplace." These plans are run by health insurance companies, but the government helps sell and administer them.

According to the Affordable Care Act ("Obamacare"), health insurance companies are not allowed to do true underwriting to determine your plan's cost. They can only price plans based on three factors: your age, your location, and whether or not you smoke. This means that government plans can often be expensive for relatively healthy people, because you are essentially subsidizing everyone else who is less healthy than you; the insurance company will have to pay much more to have them as a customer (because they need more health care), yet it has to charge them the same premium.

4. Medicare and Medicaid – These are also technically government plans, but they are free for the customer. In general, people who are above the age of sixty-five or disabled qualify for Medicare (meaning, they can get a Medicare plan for free). People beneath a certain income level qualify for Medicaid. The exact income varies by state; the average threshold is about $18,000.

Is it worth getting?

As with the liability protection from car insurance, you definitely need to protect yourself from having a nightmare scenario ruin your life (benefit #1 of health insurance).[26] If you got diagnosed with a chronic condition, or had a terrible accident, you could rack up hundreds of thousands of dollars in hospital bills.

In terms of benefit #2 of health insurance (the "subscription"), typically the answer is also yes, because it's quite difficult to pay for your health care yourself. When you do, providers will likely charge you more than what they would charge your insurance company if

---

[26] In some states, having health insurance is actually required by law: California, Massachusetts, New Jersey, Rhode Island, and Vermont. But that's not the main reason to get health insurance, because hypothetically you could pay less on the penalty than it would cost to get a health plan.

you did have coverage. However, it can be hard to know how fancy of a plan to get. If you could pay $2,000 this year for the bare minimum versus $10,000 for an all-inclusive plan, then the question is: How much health care do you think you will utilize this year?

Unfortunately, that's an almost impossible question to answer. Returning to our earlier metaphor, it's like committing to a Netflix plan before knowing if you'll even have time to watch shows that year. Because health is not a state of being—it's an estimate. You could feel perfectly healthy but be about to receive a horrible diagnosis; you could be battling a major illness now but be on the cusp of recovery.

There's no easy way to choose, other than to dive into the details of each plan that is offered, estimate how much of it you will use, then compare that to the cost of the plan. In some cases, especially if you are young and healthy, you might opt for a cheaper plan that has a very high deductible—meaning, you probably won't reach the deductible, so you are only using it as true insurance against catastrophes (hence why these plans are referred to as "catastrophic plans").

These high-deductible plans often have an additional benefit called an HSA (health savings account). Essentially, it lets you invest money tax-free, like a 401(k), except instead of being used for your retirement, the money can only be spent on health-care expenses (any time).

Either way, it's important to make sure you are always covered. If you are in between jobs, and do not choose to extend the coverage from your old job, you can find a plan via the government marketplace in the interim. Yes, it's a pain to deal with all the paperwork, but it's worth being protected.[27]

If you thought we were now done with insurance, you'd be . . . wrong! (You should get yourself "wrong guessing" insurance.) We're

27 Don't even ask me about when I went through seven different health insurance plans over the course of one year; I'm traumatized enough.

going to briefly cover two more types of insurance, before moving to taxes.

Dental insurance

In a way, dental insurance and vision insurance are even stranger than health insurance, although (mercifully) less complicated. They *do not* provide the catastrophic-coverage level of coverage, presumably because dental or eye emergencies would not result in racking up life-ruining high bills; rather, they *only* provide the subscription service for dental or eye care.

What does it cover?

Like health insurance, most dental plans have a network of providers (dentists) who are covered, and sometimes they have a deductible. After you meet the deductible, they typically have the "100/80/50 rule" for coinsurance:

- 100% of preventative care (such as routine cleanings and checkups) are covered.
- 80% of basic procedures (such as fillings) are covered, meaning you pay 20% of the cost.
- 50% of major procedures (such as crowns) are covered.

How much does it cost?

The average cost is about $400 to $800/year. Like health insurance, it is often subsidized by employers, and the premiums are tax-deductible.

Is it worth getting?

Unlike health insurance, there's no equivalent of the "catastrophic plan." So if you add up your estimated dental costs for the year, and they are lower than the cost of the plan your employer offers, then you can skip it.

Of course, it's difficult to know what your dental costs will be. Dentists recommend getting a cleaning and checkup every six months. How much do those cost? The only way to know is to call your dentist and find out. Be sure to ask how much they would charge for a cleaning and checkup if you had a certain plan versus paying yourself (the prices are usually different).

Vision insurance

What does it cover?
Vision insurance typically covers getting one eye exam per year, plus some kind of reimbursement on contact lenses and glasses.

How much does it cost?
Typically between $50 to $250 per year. Again, it's often subsidized by your employer and tax-deductible.

Is it worth getting?
Optometrists recommend getting one eye exam per year. So, you can call eye care places to ask how much they charge for an exam. Then, if you wear glasses or contacts, add the cost of what you would spend on getting new ones this year. If the total number is higher than the cost of the plan, it's worth it. (Our family saves a bit of money by getting vision insurance, if we need to buy a new pair of glasses that year anyway.)

You are finally ready to tackle taxes

There are many different kinds of taxes you pay, such as sales tax (on items you buy) and property tax (if you own a home). In this section we will focus only on **income tax**: tax you pay on the money you earn.

But, surprise! There are actually five types of income tax:

1. Social Security tax – You pay 6.2% of your income, and your employer pays an additional 6.2% from their own money. (If you are self-employed, you pay the full 12.4% yourself.) The money goes to the federal government, into their Social Security fund. You may recall from the last chapter that this is the fund that pays current retirees (so, essentially, you are funding retirees as you work).

Note that this tax has an income cap of $168,600 (as of 2024); you don't pay Social Security tax on any income you earn above the first $168,600.

2. Medicare tax – You pay 1.45% of your income, and your employer pays an additional 1.45% from their own money. (If you are self-employed, you pay the full 2.9% yourself.) The money goes to the federal government, into their Medicare fund. As we just learned, this is the fund that provides elderly and disabled people with subsidized health insurance.

3. Federal income tax – You pay a percentage of your income to the federal government. In the United States we have a "progressive" income tax, meaning the percentage you have to pay is higher the more money you earn. At right are the 2024 **tax brackets** (income tax amounts) for an unmarried person:

Tax rate	Single filers
10%	$11,600 or less
12%	$11,601 – $47,150
22%	$47,151 – $100,525
24%	$100,526 – $191,950
32%	$191,951 – $243,725
35%	$243,726 – $609,350
37%	$609,351 or more

Let's say you earn $40,000 in one year. You'd pay 10% of the first $11,600 (which is $1,160), plus 12% of the income above $11,600 (so 12% of $28,400, which is $3,408)—for a grand total of $4,568. In reality, you probably wouldn't owe the full $4,568, because the federal income tax allows you to take all kinds of deductions and exemptions. We'll dive into that shortly.

4. State income tax – You pay a percentage of your income to your state government. Some states have a progressive tax rate, others have a proportional tax rate (the same percentage for everyone), and some have no state income tax at all.[28]

If you move between states during the year, you'll have to pay income tax in each state you lived, typically proportional to the amount of time you spent there.

5. Local income tax – Some big cities (such as New York City) charge a city income tax. And some states (such as Pennsylvania) have both the state income tax (3.07%) plus a county tax (1 to 4%, depending on which county you live in).

How to pay taxes

Typically, your employer pays your income taxes for you. When they subtract a tax payment from your salary to pay the tax for you, it's called **withholding**.

Whenever you get paid, which is typically every one or two weeks, you'll receive a **pay stub**. It's essentially a receipt that shows you how much you earned, how much was deducted for your benefits, such as health insurance premiums and 401(k) contributions, and how much was withheld for taxes.

In order to know how much tax to pay on your behalf, your employer needs to estimate how much you will earn over the course of the year. They can do that based on your salary, but they need some help from you—they need info on any additional income you or a spouse may be earning, and what kind of tax deductions and credits you are eligible for. They collect this information on a **W-4 form**, a little worksheet. You'll typically be given one on your first day of work. (Note that this is separate from the I-9 form you typically need

28 Lucky you, residents of Alaska, Florida, Nevada, New Hampshire, South Dakota, Tennessee, Texas, Washington, and Wyoming!

to fill out to demonstrate that you are legally authorized to work in the United States.)

Okay, so after you fill out the W-4, your employer handles paying and tracking your taxes, so that's it, right? Wrong! (You *really* should have purchased that "guessing wrong" insurance.)

At the end of each year, you need to calculate *yourself* how much income you earned and how much federal income tax you owe (tax type #3 from our previous list). Often, there ends up being a discrepancy between how much tax your employer withheld and how much you truly owe. If you paid too little, you now need to pay the difference; if you paid too much, the government owes you a **tax refund**.

You do this calculation on a **1040 form**, which you then submit to the IRS (the Internal Revenue Service, which is the agency of the federal government that handles taxes). This is called your **tax return**.[29]

In order to fill it out, you need one master pay stub that shows your earnings and withholdings over the course of an entire year—essentially all of your pay stubs added together—which is called a **W-2 form** (not to be confused with the W-4!). Your employer typically sends your W-2 by January 31, and your tax return is typically due by April 15.

For example, in January of 2026 you will receive a W-2 from each employer you had in 2025, you will use that information to fill out the 2025 tax return, and you will submit it by April 15, 2026.

There are separate forms, which are different in each state, that you also need to fill out in order to file your state and/or local tax return.[30] For example, in Massachusetts it's called the "Form 1."

There are three ways you can do your annual tax return:

---

29 It's *not* called a return because the government "returns" some of your money (sometimes you have to pay *them* more money); rather, it's because you are "returning" a notice with information to the government.

30 And if you lived in multiple states that year, you need to fill out multiple of those!

1. DIY – Fill it out by hand, or digitally in a PDF, yourself.

2. Software – You can use a program to help you. For example, TurboTax asks you step-by-step questions, then uses that information to fill out the forms.

3. Professionals – You can hire an accountant to do it all for you. Firms like H&R Block charge a rate based on how complex your tax situation is. If it's relatively straightforward, it can cost as little as $150; if it's complicated, it can be $1,000 or more.

I highly recommend filling out the 1040 form yourself, by hand, at least once. It's the only way to truly understand how income tax works. The more deeply you understand it, the better you can optimize your finances each year to lower how much you need to pay in taxes.

Before we walk through the 1040 form in detail to understand all those possible optimizations, let's first answer some questions that are probably on the tip of your tongue:

- What happens if I make a mistake on my tax return? – Typically, the IRS will notice the mistake, correct it, and send you the corrected info along with how much more you owe (or with the money they owe you).
- If the IRS knows how much I really owe anyway, why do they make me do it all myself??? – Honestly, I'm not sure if three question marks are enough for that one. The first time this occurred to me, I was more like ???????

  Think about how much time is wasted each year, by each person in the United States—not to mention all the money that gets spent on software and professional tax-preparation services—to fill out a form that the IRS could be filling out for us! However, it's worth noting that the IRS does *not* do these calculations for everyone. They randomly select some tax returns to double-check, presumably because they do not have the time to check it for everyone.[31]

Note that this double-checking or correcting is not the same as getting audited. Being audited happens when the IRS notices major issues with your tax returns, and decides to investigate you. They'll ask for your tax records going back for up to seven years and try to determine how much tax you owe (plus interest), and whether you willfully committed fraud.

- So if I have to reconcile what I owe at the end of each year, why does my employer withhold taxes from each paycheck? Why not just pay the taxes once? – Because the government wants to collect income more than just once per year.
- What if I'm self-employed or do gig work? – In that case, you need to pay income tax four times per year, not just once. At the end of each quarter (every three months), you file a mini–tax return via form 1040-ES. And keep in mind, you will likely pay more in tax than you would if you had an employer, because you will pay the employer portion of the Social Security and Medicare taxes yourself.

All right, take a look at your watch. What time is it? 10:40 exactly!

---

31 According to research by ProPublica, another reason the IRS does not fill out your tax return themselves is that big companies like H&R Block and Intuit (which owns TurboTax) lobby the government to prevent this, so that they can continue to sell their tax-prep services.

1040 time

Here is a screenshot of the first section of the 1040 (the 2023 version), followed by an explanation. We'll walk through each section of the form in detail.

Form **1040** Department of the Treasury—Internal Revenue Service
U.S. Individual Income Tax Return **2023** OMB No. 1545-0074 IRS Use Only—Do not write or staple in this space.

For the year Jan. 1–Dec. 31, 2023, or other tax year beginning , 2023, ending , 20 See separate instructions.

Your first name and middle initial	Last name	**Your social security number**
If joint return, spouse's first name and middle initial	Last name	**Spouse's social security number**

Home address (number and street). If you have a P.O. box, see instructions.			Apt. no.	**Presidential Election Campaign** Check here if you, or your spouse if filing jointly, want $3 to go to this fund. Checking a box below will not change your tax or refund. ☐ **You** ☐ **Spouse**
City, town, or post office. If you have a foreign address, also complete spaces below.	State	ZIP code		
Foreign country name	Foreign province/state/county	Foreign postal code		

Filing Status Check only one box.
☐ Single
☐ Married filing jointly (even if only one had income)
☐ Married filing separately (MFS)
☐ Head of household (HOH)
☐ Qualifying surviving spouse (QSS)
If you checked the MFS box, enter the name of your spouse. If you checked the HOH or QSS box, enter the child's name if the qualifying person is a child but not your dependent:

Digital Assets At any time during 2023, did you: (a) receive (as a reward, award, or payment for property or services); or (b) sell, exchange, or otherwise dispose of a digital asset (or a financial interest in a digital asset)? (See instructions.) ☐ **Yes** ☐ **No**

Standard Deduction **Someone can claim:** ☐ You as a dependent ☐ Your spouse as a dependent
☐ Spouse itemizes on a separate return or you were a dual-status alien

Age/Blindness **You:** ☐ Were born before January 2, 1959 ☐ Are blind **Spouse:** ☐ Was born before January 2, 1959 ☐ Is blind

Dependents (see instructions): If more than four dependents, see instructions and check here . . ☐

(1) First name	Last name	(2) Social security number	(3) Relationship to you	(4) Check the box if qualifies for (see instructions): Child tax credit	Credit for other dependents
				☐	☐
				☐	☐
				☐	☐
				☐	☐

Your "filing status" is typically either single (yourself) or married. If you're married, you only need to file one tax return for the two of you; essentially, you pay your taxes together (aww, how romantic). The rest of this section is mostly filling out personal info, including your dependents (children).

Income	Line	Description		Box
Attach Form(s) W-2 here. Also attach Forms W-2G and 1099-R if tax was withheld.	1a	Total amount from Form(s) W-2, box 1 (see instructions)		1a
	b	Household employee wages not reported on Form(s) W-2		1b
	c	Tip income not reported on line 1a (see instructions)		1c
	d	Medicaid waiver payments not reported on Form(s) W-2 (see instructions)		1d
	e	Taxable dependent care benefits from Form 2441, line 26		1e
	f	Employer-provided adoption benefits from Form 8839, line 29		1f
If you did not get a Form W-2, see instructions.	g	Wages from Form 8919, line 6		1g
	h	Other earned income (see instructions)		1h
	i	Nontaxable combat pay election (see instructions)	1i	
	z	Add lines 1a through 1h		1z
Attach Sch. B if required.	2a	Tax-exempt interest	2a	b Taxable interest — 2b
	3a	Qualified dividends	3a	b Ordinary dividends — 3b
Standard Deduction for—	4a	IRA distributions	4a	b Taxable amount — 4b
• Single or Married filing separately, $13,850	5a	Pensions and annuities	5a	b Taxable amount — 5b
• Married filing jointly or Qualifying surviving spouse, $27,700	6a	Social security benefits	6a	b Taxable amount — 6b
• Head of household, $20,800	c	If you elect to use the lump-sum election method, check here (see instructions) ☐		
• If you checked any box under *Standard Deduction*, see instructions.	7	Capital gain or (loss). Attach Schedule D if required. If not required, check here ☐		7
	8	Additional income from Schedule 1, line 10		8
	9	Add lines 1z, 2b, 3b, 4b, 5b, 6b, 7, and 8. This is your **total income**		9
	10	Adjustments to income from Schedule 1, line 26		10
	11	Subtract line 10 from line 9. This is your **adjusted gross income**		11
	12	**Standard deduction or itemized deductions** (from Schedule A)		12
	13	Qualified business income deduction from Form 8995 or Form 8995-A		13
	14	Add lines 12 and 13		14
	15	Subtract line 14 from line 11. If zero or less, enter -0-. This is your **taxable income**		15

As you can see, you are required to add up all the income from not only all of your W-2s (the end-of-year pay stubs from each employer), but also from any as-of-yet unreported earnings, such as tips.

This section is where you also report income from investments, namely interest (line 2), dividends (line 3), and capital gains (line 7). (Remember those terms from last chapter?) As you can see, if you have certain types of income, you are required to fill out additional forms, called "schedules," and attach them to the 1040.

Line 12 is a big deduction. How exciting! A **tax deduction** is an amount of money that gets deducted (subtracted) from your income before taxes are calculated. For example, if your annual income was $60,000 and you take the standard deduction of $14,600, then your taxable income will be $45,400. That $14,600 would have been taxed at 22%, so the deduction is essentially saving you $3,212 in taxes.

Instead of taking the standard deduction of $14,600, you can instead choose to "itemize" your deductions, using Schedule A. Itemized deductions include:

- Donations to charity[32]
- State and local taxes that you paid
- Interest you paid on your mortgage
- Certain health-care expenses

So, you can first fill out Schedule A and see: Did those things add up to more than $14,600? If so, put that number in line 12 of the 1040. If not, toss out the Schedule A and just keep the standard deduction. The vast majority of people take the standard deduction.

Prior to 2018, there were plenty of other deductions one could take *in addition to* the standard deduction, including: moving expenses, unreimbursed business expenses, a home office, student-loan interest, and more. However, the Tax Cuts and Jobs Act of 2017 phased these out until the end of 2025. We'll have to wait until 2026 to see if they bring back any other deductions.

Now you know what someone means when they tell you "this is tax-deductible"—it does *not* mean free money. It means that if, for example, your tax rate is 22%, then making a tax-deductible donation of $100 will really only cost you $78 (you'll get $22 back when you file your tax return, because $100 will be deducted from your income).

Tax and Credits	**16**	**Tax** (see instructions). Check if any from Form(s): **1** ☐ 8814 **2** ☐ 4972 **3** ☐ ______	16	
	17	Amount from Schedule 2, line 3	17	
	18	Add lines 16 and 17	18	
	19	Child tax credit or credit for other dependents from Schedule 8812	19	
	20	Amount from Schedule 3, line 8	20	
	21	Add lines 19 and 20	21	
	22	Subtract line 21 from line 18. If zero or less, enter -0-	22	
	23	Other taxes, including self-employment tax, from Schedule 2, line 21	23	
	24	Add lines 22 and 23. This is your **total tax**	24	

In order to calculate the tax on line 16, you need to look up the "tax table" from the 1040 form's instructions (also available on the IRS website).

32 Note that if you want to itemize donations to charity, you must keep receipts for your donations. You don't need to submit the receipts with your 1040, but you need to have them handy in case the IRS ever asks for them.

For example, this is one snippet of the tax table from 2023.

If line 15 (taxable income) is—		And you are—			
At least	But less than	Single	Married filing jointly *	Married filing sepa-rately	Head of a house-hold
		Your tax is—			
60,000					
60,000	60,050	8,513	6,763	8,513	6,907
60,050	60,100	8,524	6,769	8,524	6,918
60,100	60,150	8,535	6,775	8,535	6,929
60,150	60,200	8,546	6,781	8,546	6,940
60,200	60,250	8,557	6,787	8,557	6,951
60,250	60,300	8,568	6,793	8,568	6,962
60,300	60,350	8,579	6,799	8,579	6,973
60,350	60,400	8,590	6,805	8,590	6,984
60,400	60,450	8,601	6,811	8,601	6,995
60,450	60,500	8,612	6,817	8,612	7,006
60,500	60,550	8,623	6,823	8,623	7,017
60,550	60,600	8,634	6,829	8,634	7,028
60,600	60,650	8,645	6,835	8,645	7,039
60,650	60,700	8,656	6,841	8,656	7,050
60,700	60,750	8,667	6,847	8,667	7,061
60,750	60,800	8,678	6,853	8,678	7,072
60,800	60,850	8,689	6,859	8,689	7,083
60,850	60,900	8,700	6,865	8,700	7,094
60,900	60,950	8,711	6,871	8,711	7,105
60,950	61,000	8,722	6,877	8,722	7,116

All this table is doing is applying the progressive tax percentages to your taxable income number to calculate the total amount you owe.

You'll notice in line 19 that you can claim a credit for having children. A credit is different from a deduction. A **tax credit** is subtracted from the total tax you owe, not from your taxable income. For example, let's say you earned $60,000, and thus owe $8,513 in taxes. If you can take a $1,000 credit, then you will only have to pay $7,513 in taxes. The credit is the amount of money you get to keep. (By contrast, a tax *deduction* of $1,000 would reduce your taxable income to $59,000, so you'd have to pay $8,293—yielding you savings of $220, not $1,000.) Thus, tax credits are five to ten times as good as tax deductions.

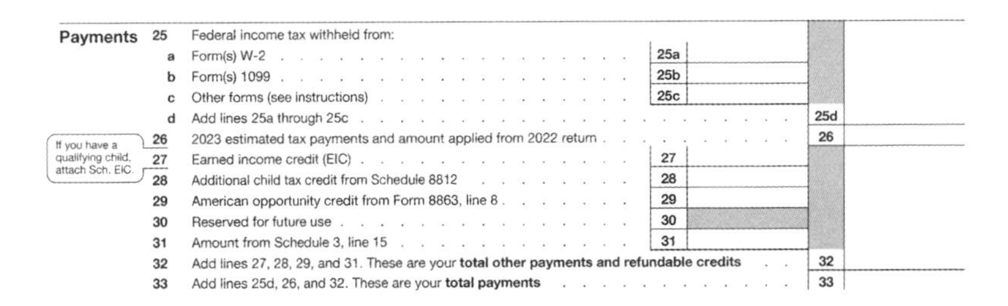

Payments

Line	Description	Box
25	Federal income tax withheld from:	
a	Form(s) W-2	25a
b	Form(s) 1099	25b
c	Other forms (see instructions)	25c
d	Add lines 25a through 25c	25d
26	2023 estimated tax payments and amount applied from 2022 return	26
27	Earned income credit (EIC)	27
28	Additional child tax credit from Schedule 8812	28
29	American opportunity credit from Form 8863, line 8	29
30	Reserved for future use	30
31	Amount from Schedule 3, line 15	31
32	Add lines 27, 28, 29, and 31. These are your **total other payments and refundable credits**	32
33	Add lines 25d, 26, and 32. These are your **total payments**	33

If you have a qualifying child, attach Sch. EIC.

Line 25 is where you share how much you've already paid in taxes throughout the year (how much your employer withheld from all your paychecks).

There are also other credits you can claim, including the earned income credit (EIC), which is intended to benefit low-income workers. The income cutoff varies depending on the number of children you have, but if you are single then you can claim the EIC if your income is less than about $16,000 (as of 2023).

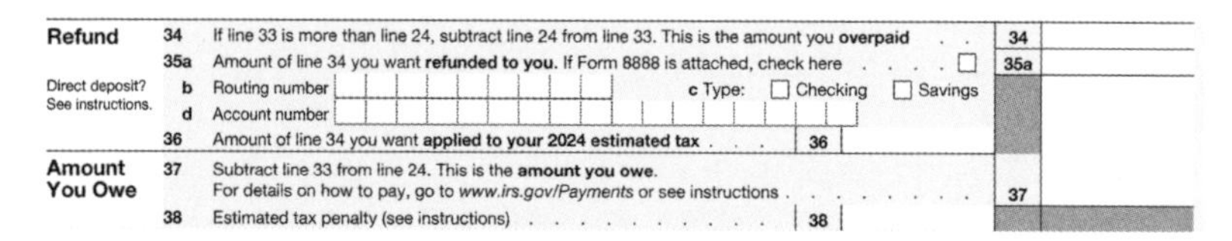

Refund	34	If line 33 is more than line 24, subtract line 24 from line 33. This is the amount you **overpaid**	34	
	35a	Amount of line 34 you want **refunded to you.** If Form 8888 is attached, check here ☐	35a	
Direct deposit? See instructions.	b	Routing number — **c** Type: ☐ Checking ☐ Savings		
	d	Account number		
	36	Amount of line 34 you want **applied to your 2024 estimated tax** — 36		
Amount You Owe	37	Subtract line 33 from line 24. This is the **amount you owe.** For details on how to pay, go to *www.irs.gov/Payments* or see instructions	37	
	38	Estimated tax penalty (see instructions) — 38		

If you paid more throughout the year than what you owe, then the IRS owes *you*. You can either input your bank info to get your refund directly deposited (if you feel comfortable sharing that information with the IRS); otherwise, they will mail you a check.

It's typically *not* worth checking the box on line 36 that will apply your refund to what you owe on next year's taxes. Because, like the IRS, you would rather have money now than later.

If you owe money, then you'll write a check and attach it to your 1040 (or, if submitting online, you'll fill out payment information).

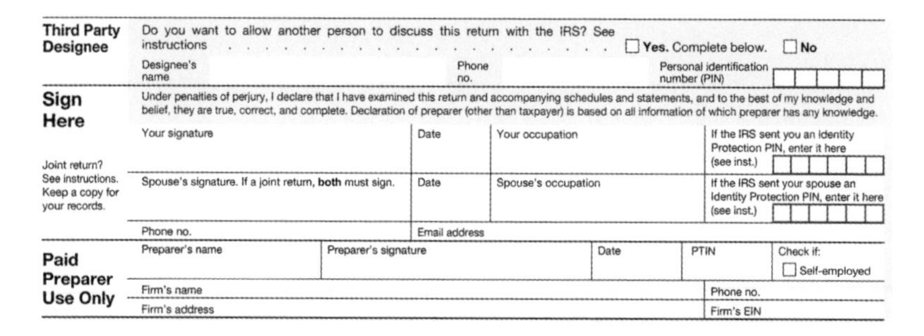

Third Party Designee
Do you want to allow another person to discuss this return with the IRS? See instructions ☐ **Yes.** Complete below. ☐ **No**
Designee's name | Phone no. | Personal identification number (PIN)

Sign Here
Under penalties of perjury, I declare that I have examined this return and accompanying schedules and statements, and to the best of my knowledge and belief, they are true, correct, and complete. Declaration of preparer (other than taxpayer) is based on all information of which preparer has any knowledge.
Your signature | Date | Your occupation | If the IRS sent you an Identity Protection PIN, enter it here (see inst.)
Joint return? See instructions. Keep a copy for your records.
Spouse's signature. If a joint return, **both** must sign. | Date | Spouse's occupation | If the IRS sent your spouse an Identity Protection PIN, enter it here (see inst.)
Phone no. | Email address

Paid Preparer Use Only
Preparer's name | Preparer's signature | Date | PTIN | Check if: ☐ Self-employed
Firm's name | Phone no.
Firm's address | Firm's EIN

There's no need to fill out the third-party designee info (or the "paid preparer use only") unless you are having someone else, such as an accountant, do your taxes for you.

Lastly, do not forget to sign it! I once felt so proud of completing my tax return myself that I forgot to sign it. The IRS returned it to me, which was super embarrassing, of course, plus it delayed getting my tax refund.

You can either submit your tax return by mail, or online ("e-file"). If you mail it, you must staple it on the top-left corner, then staple a copy of each of your W-2s to the top-right corner. This constantly confused me, so here's a diagram that should help:

This staple goes through all pages of the 1040 and all schedules

This staple goes through ONLY the first page of the 1040, and all of your W-2s (which are usually small squares of paper)

Form **1040** Department of the Treasury—Internal Revenue Service
U.S. Individual Income Tax Return **2023** OMB No. 1545-0074 IRS Use Only—Do not write or staple in this space.

For the year Jan. 1–Dec. 31, 2023, or other tax year beginning , 2023, ending , 20 See separate instructions.

Your first name and middle initial | Last name | **Your social security number**

If joint return, spouse's first name and middle initial | Last name | **Spouse's social security number**

Home address (number and street). If you have a P.O. box, see instructions. | Apt. no. | **Presidential Election Campaign** Check here if you, or your spouse if filing jointly, want $3 to go to this fund. Checking a box below will not change your tax or refund. ☐ You ☐ Spouse

City, town, or post office. If you have a foreign address, also complete spaces below. | State | ZIP code

Foreign country name | Foreign province/state/county | Foreign postal code

Filing Status Check only one box. ☐ Single ☐ Married filing jointly (even if only one had income) ☐ Married filing separately (MFS) ☐ Head of household (HOH) ☐ Qualifying surviving spouse (QSS)
If you checked the MFS box, enter the name of your spouse. If you checked the HOH or QSS box, enter the child's name if the qualifying person is a child but not your dependent:

Digital Assets At any time during 2023, did you: (a) receive (as a reward, award, or payment for property or services); or (b) sell, exchange, or otherwise dispose of a digital asset (or a financial interest in a digital asset)? (See instructions.) ☐ Yes ☐ No

Standard Deduction **Someone can claim:** ☐ You as a dependent ☐ Your spouse as a dependent
☐ Spouse itemizes on a separate return or you were a dual-status alien

Age/Blindness **You:** ☐ Were born before January 2, 1959 ☐ Are blind **Spouse:** ☐ Was born before January 2, 1959 ☐ Is blind

Dependents (see instructions): If more than four dependents, see instructions and check here ☐

(1) First name Last name	(2) Social security number	(3) Relationship to you	(4) Check the box if qualifies for (see instructions): Child tax credit	Credit for other dependents
			☐	☐
			☐	☐
			☐	☐
			☐	☐

Income
Attach Form(s) W-2 here. Also attach Forms W-2G and 1099-R if tax was withheld.
If you did not get a Form W-2, see instructions.

1a Total amount from Form(s) W-2, box 1 (see instructions) 1a
b Household employee wages not reported on Form(s) W-2 1b
c Tip income not reported on line 1a (see instructions) 1c
d Medicaid waiver payments not reported on Form(s) W-2 (see instructions) 1d
e Taxable dependent care benefits from Form 2441, line 26 1e
f Employer-provided adoption benefits from Form 8839, line 29 1f
g Wages from Form 8919, line 6 1g
h Other earned income (see instructions) 1h
i Nontaxable combat pay election (see instructions) 1i
z Add lines 1a through 1h 1z

Attach Sch. B if required.
2a Tax-exempt interest 2a | b Taxable interest 2b
3a Qualified dividends 3a | b Ordinary dividends 3b
4a IRA distributions 4a | b Taxable amount 4b
5a Pensions and annuities 5a | b Taxable amount 5b
6a Social security benefits 6a | b Taxable amount 6b
c If you elect to use the lump-sum election method, check here (see instructions) ☐
7 Capital gain or (loss). Attach Schedule D if required. If not required, check here ☐ 7
8 Additional income from Schedule 1, line 10 8
9 Add lines 1z, 2b, 3b, 4b, 5b, 6b, 7, and 8. This is your **total income** 9
10 Adjustments to income from Schedule 1, line 26 10
11 Subtract line 10 from line 9. This is your **adjusted gross income** 11
12 **Standard deduction or itemized deductions** (from Schedule A) 12
13 Qualified business income deduction from Form 8995 or Form 8995-A 13
14 Add lines 12 and 13 14
15 Subtract line 14 from line 11. If zero or less, enter -0-. This is your **taxable income** 15

Standard Deduction for—
• Single or Married filing separately, $13,850
• Married filing jointly or Qualifying surviving spouse, $27,700
• Head of household, $20,800
• If you checked any box under Standard Deduction, see instructions.

For Disclosure, Privacy Act, and Paperwork Reduction Act Notice, see separate instructions. Cat. No. 11320B Form **1040** (2023)

Also, remember to keep (at least) one printed and/or digital copy of your tax return! You are required to keep these records for seven years; if you ever get audited, the IRS will ask to see them. Also, if they need to make a minor correction to your return, you can refer to your own copy to make sure everything checks out.[33]

And that's it! So, what will doing all this yourself likely teach you?

- All your income must be reported. Even if you earn something under the table, you will be legally required to report that on your 1040 and pay taxes on it. There's no such thing as tax-free income!
- It's only worth racking up deductions like donations to charity *if* you think you will exceed the standard deduction each year. Otherwise, they won't help you for tax purposes.[34]
- Credits are much better than deductions. In the past, you could claim a certain type of deduction or credit for educational expenses. It's helpful to understand the difference, in case any options like that reappear in the tax code, so you can calculate which will yield you more savings.

---

33 One year I forgot to make a copy, and the IRS made a mistake in *their* correction: They added an extra zero to my income, thinking I was quite rich! I wanted to prove that was not what I submitted; however, I didn't have a copy to show them. So, I had to redo the *entire* thing by hand.

34 My wife and I donate 10% of our annual income to charity. But, we try to stagger our donations so that we can exceed the standard deduction. For example, around January 2026 we will donate 10% of what our income was in 2025; in December, we will donate 10% of what our (estimated) income was in 2026. That way, we can beat the standard deduction on our 2026 tax return. In 2027, we will take the standard deduction, then repeat in 2028.

SUMMARY

- The purpose of insurance is to avoid having a disaster ruin you financially; you pay a regular premium so that if the disaster happens, you'll receive a payout (minus the deductible).
- Car insurance covers many things, the most important of which is liability (bodily injury and property damage) in case someone sues you; it's typically worth getting coverage of at least $100,000 for each.
- Renters' insurance protects the things you own; if you cannot afford to re-buy all of them, it's worth purchasing.
- Life insurance and disability insurance are typically only worth getting if you have people who depend on your income.
- Health insurance is really two things in one: (1) protection against catastrophic medical bills, and (2) a health-care services subscription; it's always worth having #1, and #2 could be worth paying extra for (a plan with a lower deductible) if you anticipate spending enough on health care that year.
- You must pay five types of income tax: Social Security, Medicare, federal, state, and (sometimes) local.
- Although income gets withheld from each paycheck, you must still reconcile it by filing a tax return (1040 form) each year; do not forget to sign it, staple it, and keep a copy.

Homework

IF YOU DRIVE . . . Get car insurance! Find an insurance agent or use an online marketplace. If you already have car insurance, check your coverage levels across all seven categories. If you need to increase your coverage (especially for bodily injury and property damage), contact your insurance company. You can also try to use some of the tactics described earlier to lower your premium.

IF YOU OWN STUFF . . . Get renters' insurance. Find an insurance agent or use an online marketplace. If you already have it, check your coverage level to make sure it matches the estimated value of all the stuff you would need to replace. Film your possessions so you have a record of them.

IF YOU HAVE A BODY . . . You probably already have health insurance. If it's through your parents, ask them to show you the policy so you can better understand what's covered and how much the deductible, copays and coinsurances, out-of-pocket limit, and maximum lifetime benefit are. If you get health insurance through your employer, similarly review your policy (you can email the human resources department to ask for that info). If you do not have health insurance, and cannot obtain it through an employer or a parent, go to healthcare.gov to shop for a government-provided plan.

IF YOU WORK . . . Review your latest pay stub. Note how much is being deducted for benefits such as health insurance, and how much is being withheld for all five types of income tax.

Extra credit: The next time you must file a tax return (before mid-April each calendar year), assuming that your tax situation is not too complex, fill out the 1040 form by hand.

Skill #8

STICK TO A BUDGET

When I was a kid, my mother and grandfather planned a surprise activity for my brother and me. First, we did little art projects like drawing a cartoon or building a small craft. We "sold" this work to my mom for play money. Then, she laid out a row of prizes we could buy: a notebook, a night-light, toys. Each of us had enough money to buy a couple trinkets. After deciding, we noticed that my grandfather didn't buy anything; he saved his money.

We had another round of producing artwork, selling it, then getting to buy things. Again, my grandfather kept his cash. A few rounds later, my mom brought a new good to the market: a massive chocolate bar. It must have weighed at least one pound; it put the trinkets we had purchased to shame. The chocolate's price: more than any of us had earned for selling our artwork that round. "But it's too much! We couldn't buy it even if we wanted to!" we protested.

My grandfather said, "I can." He pulled out the pretend cash he had saved, and go figure, it was exactly enough to afford the chocolate. (The valuable lesson on saving was somewhat diminished when my grandfather—unable to suppress his kind instincts—shared his spoils with us.)

Even though we know we should be saving because we want to buy the proverbial chocolate—whether it's something indulgent like a vacation, or something practical like a down payment on a house—it can be extremely difficult to save in practice. The solution is budgeting: deciding in advance how much to spend so we can allocate the rest for savings.

But how do we decide what should fit into the budget and what we can do without? Here's a personal experience that blew my mind. At my first full-time job, there was a cafeteria that sold packaged Naked smoothies. For just $4 a day, I could taste that sweet, sweet mango-orange concoction. On a generous salary of $70,000, $4 each day seemed like nothing. But then I realized: There are about 250 workdays in a year, so the smoothies cost $1,000/year. Taxes already ate my salary down to $45,000, and paying rent brought it down further to $27,000 (New York apartments are crazy expensive). So that's almost 4% of my disposable income—before even allocating for savings—just for one Naked drink per workday!

That isn't to say you should feel guilty about spending regularly on something that brings you pleasure. In fact, the most important principle of budgeting is . . .

Your budget doesn't confine you, it liberates you

Without a budget, every purchase you make could be a struggle: "Is it really worth spending another $5 per month to get the softer toilet paper?" You're prey to constant agonizing, including feeling guilty when you do spend. Spending on things you like shouldn't bring you guilt; it should bring you pleasure!

That's why planning a budget liberates you. You say in advance, "I can spend $300 on nonessential expenses this month." Then, when there's something you want to buy, it comes out of the $300, and you aren't left worrying that you won't have enough to pay rent this month or invest for your retirement.

Self-imposed restrictions give you the freedom to spend within those restrictions. You can always reevaluate every year how much you've allocated for certain types of spending, and whether it's worth raising or lowering that amount for next year.

So, are you ready to be liberated?

What follows is a template I created that aims to be as comprehensive as possible. It includes most expenses young people could likely have, each in its own row. The goal is to come up with an annual budget. In some cases, it's easier to track monthly expenses, so I input those, then multiplied by twelve.

	Monthly	Annual
Income		
Full-Time Job		$ 60,000
Investment Income (interest, dividends, capital gains)		$ 500
Self-Employment		$ -
Total Income		$ 60,500
Tax-Deductible Expenses		
Health Insurance		$ 4,000
Dental Insurance		$ 400
Vision Insurance		$ 150
Other Tax-Deductible Insurance (life, disability, etc.)		$ 100
401(k) (and Traditional IRA)		$ 2,400
Taxable Income		$ 53,450
Taxes		
Social Security Tax		$ 3,720
Medicare Tax		$ 877
Federal Income Tax		$ 5,852
State Income Tax		$ 2,138
Local Income Tax		$ -
After-Tax Income		$ 40,863
Charity		
Tithe (10%)		$ 4,086
Disposable Income		$ 36,776

	Monthly	Annual
Home & Utilities		
Rent or Mortgage	$ 1,000	$ 12,000
Homeowner Expenses (repairs, HOA fees, etc.)	$ -	$ -
Electricity	$ 50	$ 600
Water	$ 25	$ 300
Gas	$ 15	$ 180
Internet	$ 60	$ 720
Phone	$ 60	$ 720
Insurance		
Car Insurance		$ 1,200
Life Insurance		$ -
Property Insurance (renters' or homeowners')		$ 150
Debt		
Student Loans	$ 200	$ 2,400
Car Payments (if leased)	$ 120	$ 1,440
Credit Card Interest Payments	$ -	$ -
Other Loans	$ -	$ -
Transportation		
Gas	$ 50	$ 600
Parking	$ 50	$ 600
Car Maintenance & Repairs	$ 100	$ 1,200
Public Transit (subway, bus, etc.)	$ 20	$ 240
Rideshares & Taxis	$ 50	$ 600
Health Care		
Health Care (doctor's appointments, ER visits, etc.)		$ 1,000
Dental Care		$ 250
Medicine		$ 100
Personal Care		
Gym Memberships	$ 40	$ 480
Haircuts & Styling	$ 30	$ 360
Cosmetics	$ 25	$ 300

	Monthly	Annual
Necessities		
Groceries	$ 250	$ 3,000
Home Supplies (toilet paper, cleaning, etc.)	$ 30	$ 360
Clothing	$ 40	$ 480
Laundry	$ 15	$ 180
Pet Care (food, supplies)	$ 70	$ 840
—		
Remaining		$ 6,476
Entertainment		
Eating Out	$ 80	$ 960
Movies & Concerts	$ 20	$ 240
Drinks	$ 50	$ 600
Streaming & Cable	$ 15	$ 180
Software & Apps	$ 5	$ 60
Books & Newspaper/Magazine Subscriptions	$ 10	$ 120
Hobbies	$ 50	$ 600
Gifts (for others)	$ 30	$ 360
Travel		
Vacations		$ 1,200
Savings		
Emergency Fund		$ 1,500
Retirement (IRA)		$ 500
Short-Term Investments		$ -
—		
Leftover		$ 156

Based on this example, you can create your own spreadsheet. Some tips:

- Review your prior pay stubs to get accurate numbers for your income and taxes, and review the past few months of your bank transaction history to get estimates for the rest.
- You can consolidate some rows to simplify the spreadsheet. For example, you can lump all tax-deductible insurance expenses into one line, if that makes it easier for you to track.
- Once you've input an honest estimate of everything you spend that's necessary—everything above the entertainment line—whatever remains can be allocated between entertainment, travel, and savings.
- What is a necessity versus a luxury? Is spending an extra $5 per month to get the nicer toilet paper *necessary*? You can always start by calculating the spending that's truly necessary to keep your life going, then reallocating whatever money remains. For example, you could start with $30 a month on home supplies, but if you have budget remaining, then you can increase it to $35/month and see how it impacts the bottom line.
- In terms of allocating toward savings, you can follow the plan we laid out at the end of skill #6. To recap, this was the order of priorities:

    1. Insurance
    2. Pay off high-interest debt
    3. Build an emergency fund (three to six months of living expenses, in cash)
    4. Max the match on your 401(k)
    5. Max your IRA
    6. Pay off lower-interest debt
    7. Short-term investments (for a large purchase like a house)

For example, if you have extra budget remaining, you could increase your 401(k) contribution (if you aren't already maxing the match that your employer offers).

Tracking your spending

Your next step is to track your spending—every month—and compare it to what's in your budget. Then, continue to update your budget as you learn more about your actual spending.

If you realize that you're spending more on something than you'd like to (for example, on mango-orange smoothies), don't pretend it's not true. Be honest with yourself! You then have two options:

1. You can update the number in your budget to more closely mirror reality.
2. You can change your spending habit.

There is no other option! There's no point in having a budget that doesn't work in practice. It's better to have a budget that's accurate—even if the bottom line is in the red (negative)—than to have a budget that is so divorced from reality that it's unusable.

Of course, doing #2 is easier said than done. Here are some tips for sticking to a budget.

1. The three-week experiment – If you're hesitant about giving something up, try going without it for three weeks. Why three weeks? That's long enough to force you to try to work around it. Instead of just avoiding a Starbucks latte for a couple days then going back to it out of desperation, if you commit to three weeks you'll realize you may not be able to go without the caffeine, and you'll bring instant coffee to work. Instead of just not seeing friends for a few days because you're giving up Uber, you'll learn the public transportation routes.

If, after the three weeks are over, you feel like your quality of life is fine, you've established a permanent thrifty habit. If your quality of life is significantly worse, you can go back to your old purchases with a clean conscience.

2. Don't compare – You may see your friends casually laying down double the drinks budget that you have, or planning a vacation that's three times as much as your average. You may even know that they have a similar income to you. Thus, you may reason, "If they can afford it, so can I."

That line of thinking is a trap. Perhaps they *cannot* afford it, and they are setting themselves up for financial failure. Or perhaps they can afford it, but they aren't saving up, as you are, to buy a house. Or perhaps they can afford it, and *you* cannot, because you spend twice as much as they do on movie tickets (guilty as charged).

3. Calculate as a percentage of leisure budget – If you are considering splurging on something, you may be tempted to calculate the expense as a percentage of your total salary. For example, on a $60,000 salary, a $300 concert is only 0.05% of your total earnings. Surely you can afford that!

But that percentage is misleading, since you cannot spend all $60,000 on whatever you want. There are taxes, as well as necessary expenses (like insurance). Instead, look at the total amount in your entertainment and vacation lines. (In the above budget example, it's $4,320, so a $300 ticket is almost 7% of your *annual* budget.) You may still determine it's worth it to you, but you'll more clearly understand how that decision impacts your remaining entertainment and vacation budget for the year.[35]

---

35 I should have done this for my Naked smoothie habit! It may have been 4% of my post-tax, post-rent income, but I wasn't accounting for all my other necessary expenses. They were probably more than 20% of my leisure budget.

4. Containment – "I just dropped $50 at a fancy restaurant last night, so at this point I might as well spend another $50 for the fancier groceries today." No! You can think of that overspending as a little virus in your budget. You don't want it spreading and getting the rest of your budget sick; contain it.

If you have a weakness for something, you can accept that you're going to spend more on it, and update your budget accordingly—not use it as justification for further spending.

5. Consider the money-to-happiness ratio – Sometimes unexpected expenses come up, and you have to dip into your savings. That's okay! Especially if it's for something very important, like health care.

My friend was debating whether it was worth following up with a dentist appointment that she knew would be expensive. My advice was: It's absolutely worth the money. Spending on your health is probably the best possible use of money. If you don't have your health, it's harder to enjoy everything else. No other use of $200—clothing, fine dining—could bring you as much happiness as the $200 for not having a toothache.

Most people's utility functions are logarithmic when it comes to money. That's a fancy way of saying: The more money you have, the less happiness each additional dollar can bring you. Without enough money for basic necessities, you'd be miserable. And going from having no shelter to having an apartment is worth way more to you than going from one apartment to a nicer one that costs twice as much.

In the same way, you can prioritize your budget based on how much happiness each allocation brings you. If visiting a faraway friend means a lot to you, then even if it's very expensive, you don't need to feel guilty about spending money on it. A $1,000 trip may bring you much more happiness than 250 $4 drinks, or it may not. Everyone's dollars are worth different amounts to them.

6. Be grateful for your bills – This may feel like a stretch, but I think it's worth considering. The next time you pay your electric bill, try not to think, "Darn, there goes $50 for something as basic as electricity," but rather, "I *get* to power my lights, refrigerator, and electronics. These are incredible modern luxuries! And I'm proud to earn enough money, on my own, to afford them."

We often think of bills as something we "have" to pay—and true, I have been referring to them as necessities—but, as we'll explore further in skill #14, you don't *have* to pay them . . . You could splurge on a big vacation and live without electricity for a few months. It's just that you probably don't *want* to. So, might as well remember that in the moment (when you're paying the bill) to get that jolt of gratitude.

When it comes to saving up for large purchases, most people assume they will need to buy a house at some point. The conventional wisdom goes: "When you rent, your rent payments are throwing away money. When you own, your mortgage payments are an investment. And houses are the best kind of investment."

Is that true? It's complicated! Buying a house is a prime example of financial advice from your parents' generation that may not apply to yours . . .

Renting versus buying

As with any kind of spending, the question is always, "What else could you be doing with that money?" If you're considering buying a house as an investment, you could instead invest that money elsewhere, such as in an S&P 500 index fund.

It's worth noting that many of the costs associated with homeownership are also "throwing money away" (getting a temporary benefit out of them):

1. Interest on your mortgage
2. Maintenance and repairs (which a landlord would typically cover if you rent instead)
3. Property tax
4. Homeowners' insurance
5. HOA or condo fees (which a landlord would typically cover if you rent instead)

According to my research, if you were to buy instead of rent an equivalently sized home in the same area, the five costs above can easily add up to *equal* what you pay on rent. In other words, if it costs you $1,500/month to rent a house, it can often cost you $1,500/month to own a house—excluding the payments you're making toward ownership of the house (the part of your mortgage payment that goes to the principal, not interest).

When that's true, the question becomes, how does a house—as an investment—compare to the total stock market? In other words: If what you'd be spending on the five costs above would equate to the money you'd be putting into rent anyway, then if you have leftover money, is putting it into equity (ownership) of a house the best way to invest that money?

As we learned in skill #6, over the long term, the total stock market grows at an average of 9 to 10% per year. Many people assume house values always go up, but that is not the case! Imagine you bought a house in Detroit in the late 1990s. People often assume that they are savants at picking the best neighborhoods that are going to boom, but of course, as with all investments, most of it ends up being guesswork, because nobody can predict the future. The *average* home appreciation rate in the United States over the past one hundred or so years is hard to estimate (understandably so—there are a lot of houses, so it's difficult to track all of them). The most reasonable economists' estimates I've read are about 3 to 4% per year. That's a lot less than 9 to 10%.

However, we're not done yet. A house does have two major advantages as an investment:

1. Taxes – If you sell your house for a profit, the first $250,000 of those capital gains are tax-free ($500,000 if you're married). In other words, you don't have to pay capital gains tax on much of the profit from your house.[36]

2. Leverage – Most mortgages only require a 10% down payment. (For example, if you buy a house for $500,000, you only need to pay $50,000 up front, and you take a loan for the remaining 90%.) However, the *entire* house appreciates, not just 10% of it. It's as if you could invest $50,000 in the stock market, and someone would loan you another $450,000 to invest alongside it. That financial concept is called **leverage** and it adds up quickly.

Do those two benefits make up for the approximately 6% lower growth of houses (compared to the stock market)? It depends on many factors, including how long you plan to own the house. Counterintuitively, the *less* time you own the house, the better (speaking purely as an investment), because then you benefit more from the leverage.[37] The leverage is extremely powerful.

Thus, in order to calculate whether you should rent or buy, you'd need to compare the five "throwaway" ownership costs to the cost of rent, then compare the house's estimated appreciation to the total stock market. There are further wrinkles, such as the tax deduction for mortgage interest, and the high transaction costs of selling a house. (I told you it gets complicated!)

In addition, there are the nonmonetary benefits of buying: if you like the feeling of ownership, or don't like dealing with a landlord. Alternatively, some people love having a landlord so that they don't need to be responsible for fixing things themselves. We were also assuming that you'd have the discipline to invest into the stock

36 There are lots of IRS asterisks around this. The main one is that the house has to be considered your primary residence (where you live most of the time), in order to prevent professional real estate investors from taking advantage of this tax benefit.

37 This is only true up to a point, because when you sell, you incur onetime transaction costs (like paying the realtor)—so you don't want to be buying and selling houses too often.

market all the extra money you would be putting into your house. (Some people know they don't have that discipline, so for them owning a house can be a good "forcing function" to make sure they're putting some of their regular income into a long-term investment.)

On the other hand, in many respects owning a home is more risky, because you are not diversified. When so much of your net worth is tied up in the value of the home, if another real estate crash like 2008 happened, and if you had to move (let's say for job reasons), you'd have to sell the house for less than you bought it for, or even—in some extreme cases—not be able to pay back the bank.

Getting into the nitty-gritty of this decision would require an entire book of its own. And strangely, I haven't found any existing ones that go into this level of detail on the trade-offs. The bottom line is that buying versus renting is not as straightforward as the conventional wisdom.

My extremely generalized, please-don't-take-this-as-Gospel-truth recommendation is as follows: If you've decided to settle down in one spot for at least three years, and you have enough savings to afford the 10% down payment without dipping into your emergency fund, and you can afford the mortgage payments and other monthly costs associated with ownership without impacting most of the "necessities" in your budget, then buying may be worth it; and, if you really want to maximize your investment, it may be best to sell (or simply remortgage the home) within seven to ten years, so you get the most benefit from your mortgage's leverage.

What is the purpose of money?

This concludes not only our chapter about budgeting, but also our entire section about personal finance. Ultimately, I hope you've learned enough to build up your credit score, invest for retirement, get insured, pay your taxes, and budget your spending. The question remains: Why? Why do you want to prevent financial ruin, or, more broadly, accumulate more wealth over time?

The answer is actually not so obvious! Money means different things to different people. To me personally, money represents freedom; if I save up enough, I can do work that is meaningful without worrying about how much income it makes. It also represents family; the more I earn, the more I can grow my family.

No matter what money means to you, it can be a constant source of worry. There are two ways to worry less about money: Earn more, or spend less.

The final chapters in this book are about career, and they will help you with the "earn more" plan. Just be wary: Your lifestyle (how much you're spending) can quickly catch up with your latest raise. If you're not paying attention, the cycle continues—you need to earn more to keep up with your higher spending—and you've never freed yourself from the pressure. Sometimes, luxury can be worth striving for; other times, it can be a trap.

The "spend less" plan can also lead to perpetual worry, if you scrutinize each purchasing decision while thinking about your total bank balance going down each time . . . unless you make it an unconscious habit to spend beneath your means. If you "automatically" spend less than you earn, you'll be accumulating more savings each day (which equals more freedom, to me).

Thus, creating—and sticking to—a realistic budget is one of the best paths to living financially worry-free.

SUMMARY

- The purpose of budgeting is to decide in advance how much to spend so you can allocate the rest for savings.
- Once you've built a budget, track your actual spending and adjust your budget accordingly over time.
- Tips for sticking to your budget: If you want to cut a spending habit, try going for three weeks without it; don't compare your spending to anyone else's; contain your spending mistakes by not letting them be justification for further wasteful spending; consider the money-to-happiness ratio (what purchases actually bring you the most benefit?).
- It's not always better to buy a house than to rent, as long as you diligently invest whatever the difference would be.

Homework

Using the template above, build your own budget. Over the next month, carefully track your spending. At the end of the month, compare it to your budget, and make any needed adjustments.

Extra credit: Pick one thing that you think you spend too much on. Try going for three weeks without it. At the end of the three weeks, decide if you want to bring it back or not.

III.

Relationship Skills

Skill #9

HAVE GOOD CONVERSATIONS

Most of us never studied how to have conversations. Even reading that sentence probably sounds nonsensical; of course we all know how to talk—we've been doing it since age two. What can there be to learn?

Every conversation in our lives has a purpose. That purpose may not be obvious to us from the beginning, but eventually it becomes clear what the conversation was: an opportunity to get to know someone better, or to enjoy someone's company, or to help someone feel heard.

Yet we fall into most conversations without ever thinking about their purpose, and as a result we often don't act the way we wish we would have in hindsight: "I missed an opportunity there; instead, I just vented my emotions."

In this chapter, we will cover techniques to make the most of three types of conversations:

1. When you need something from someone else
2. When someone else needs something from you
3. When you disagree with someone

When you need something from someone else

When people need something, they use four different communication styles—and not all are equally effective.

1. Passive – You avoid expressing your opinions, feelings, and needs. When you do, it is softly or by being overly apologetic about it. Over time, resentment builds: You feel like others ignore you, or that they deliberately trample on your rights. Eventually, this can lead to an outburst (disproportionate to the mild thing that triggered it), followed by feelings of guilt and shame, then continued passive behavior.

2. Aggressive – You express your feelings and needs with the expectation that others will accommodate them. Thus, you interrupt others, dominate them, and are not above using tactics like humiliation and threats to control them. You feel a sense of entitlement, or superiority over other people.

3. Passive-aggressive – You appear passive but are actually acting in aggressive ways beneath the surface. You may feel the same things as an aggressive person (entitlement, superiority) but you are unable to act on those feelings overtly—and thus attack your targets behind their backs. You mutter under your breath or roll your eyes, use sarcasm, or appear cooperative while secretly undermining others.

4. Assertive – You believe that you have the right to speak your mind, and others have the right to do what they will with your opinions. You value your own needs without undermining others' needs. You use "I" statements rather than "you" statements, and you don't hesitate to state your needs and feelings clearly.

As you can probably tell, assertive communication is the best, by far. Studies have linked assertiveness to better mental health, lower stress, and even higher job satisfaction. Unfortunately, the term "assertiveness" sometimes has a negative connotation, mainly because it is often used interchangeably with "aggressiveness." But they are so different! Aggressiveness is "my way or the highway"; assertiveness is just telling people "this is my preferred way." If you don't tell people what you want, they'll never know.

Other common hesitations to being assertive:

- "I'll come across as aggressive, because they'll feel obligated to do what I say." – I'm often prone to this concern. For example, whenever I'm cold in an Uber, I get stuck because I don't want the driver to think I'm entitled to choose the temperature or to think that I somehow believe they are inferior to me. I must remember that's a common thought error committed by passive communicators—I'm assuming that the driver has no agency. I am free to state my preferences, and they are free to say, "No, sorry."
- "I'll come across as passive-aggressive." – No, being passive-aggressive comes across as passive-aggressive! It's surprisingly easy for people to spot. Being assertive is the opposite: *directly* stating your preferences, rather than waging a guerilla warfare campaign to get what you want.

Communicating well not only improves the outcome of conversations, but it can also improve your worldview. Assertive communicators often feel more in control of their lives because they are comfortable advocating for themselves, and because they recognize they cannot control others. By contrast, passive, aggressive, and passive-aggressive communicators often believe they can determine other people's behavior, and either attempt to do so (aggressive) or give up on doing so and feel powerless (passive).

Let's practice! In your notebook, for each of the following requests, reframe it to being assertive.

Practice 1.

When you're hanging out with your boyfriend and other friends, he often makes comments that undermine your intelligence. They're mostly minor, like, "Oh, you should explain that again for her," and you believe it's unintentional. Still, it's come to bother you more and more.

Your current response: Squirm internally, but say nothing.

Is this response passive, aggressive, or passive-aggressive?

Write your new, assertive response.

Here's my answer: Passive.

Reframed response: "I want to talk to you about something you said tonight. [Share specific example.] I know it may seem minor, but it does make me feel unvalued. I know you care about me and are probably doing it totally unintentionally. So I just want to request that you be mindful of it in the future."

Practice 2.

You're on a road trip with friends, but you've been getting nauseous when you're not the one driving. This morning, someone else has the keys and starts walking to the car.

Your current response: (grabbing the keys from them) "It's my turn today."

Is this response passive, aggressive, or passive-aggressive?

Write your new, assertive response.

Here's my answer: Aggressive.

Reframed response: "I know I drove recently, but could I have another turn today? Unfortunately, I've been getting nauseous sitting in the back, and it helps a lot when I drive."

Practice 3.

Every day, you bring your lunch to work and put it in the breakroom fridge. It's all labeled, but today is the second day your dessert is missing.

Your current response: Leave an anonymous note on the fridge that says, "If you're thinking of leaving your food in here, DON'T. Someone is stealing things."

Is this response passive, aggressive, or passive-aggressive?

Write your new, assertive response.

Here's my answer: Passive-aggressive.

Reframed response: Leave a note that says: "To the person who ate the dessert in the fridge today—I think you accidentally ate my food. That's okay, I know it happens. Next time, please check to see if it's labeled." [Sign the note with your name, so they know whom to talk to if they want to ask a question—or apologize.]

When it comes to communicating your wants, what if what you want is for someone to change their behavior toward you? There are two additional tactics you can use:

1. Use positive reinforcement rather than criticism – Dale Carnegie, author of the ever-popular book *How to Win Friends and Influence People*, has one golden rule: Never criticize. Criticism makes other people defensive; their instinct will be to disprove whatever you're alleging, rather than reflect on it. Instead, you can motivate using positive reinforcement: "Keep doing this good thing," or "I think you are awesome, which is why I know you're capable of more."

The "golden rule" of feedback is to give five positive comments for every one negative comment—that's a lot! And it works. First, because the positive comments help you build trust for when your feedback is more critical. Second, because the positive comments encourage people to continue that good behavior: "That was great—I would love to see even more of it."

2. Show you are on the same side – When we're delivering feedback, we often unintentionally set up an oppositional dynamic: I want you to change, and you don't; it's my word against yours; it's me against you. But in reality, when you want someone to change their behavior because you care about them, you are on the same side. You both want that person to grow and succeed. So . . . just say that! "I care about you. We both want you to grow and succeed. We are on the same side; we are on team *you*."

When someone else needs something from you

When someone asks for something you don't want to do, or when someone shares critical feedback, you may become defensive. Or—and I'm extremely prone to this one—you can jump right into trying to solve their problem. This often backfires, because if the other person feels like you haven't adequately heard them, then you don't fully understand their issue, and thus your opinions are useless.

I always try to stop myself in the moment, take a breath, and remember to use this framework for empathetic listening:

1. Acknowledge – Recognize and validate their emotions.
Helpful phrase: "That does sound frustrating."

2. Repeat – Play back what you heard, in your own words. Ask for feedback, then keep iterating until you can articulate it to their satisfaction.
Helpful phrase: "What I'm hearing you say is . . . Is that right?"

3. Share – Express how you are feeling in the moment. Per what we learned about assertiveness, there's no need to hold back—you can be honest if their comments make you sad or frustrated.
Helpful phrase: "When you said that, it made me feel . . ."

4. Solve – Now you can get into solutions. Similar to when you are giving someone else constructive feedback, remember to start with shared intent.
Helpful phrase: "It sounds like we both want . . ."

Here's an example of this in a dialogue:

Roommate: I couldn't find my keys again this morning, and I was late for work. Can you please stop rearranging everything at night?

You: Oh man, I'm sorry that happened. It sounds stressful.

Roommate: It really was. I just feel like every night I go to bed and you reorganize the apartment.

You: I want to make sure I understand the issue. You think I keep moving your keys?

Roommate: No, not necessarily. I don't know if you touched my keys, it's just that when everything else is in a different place it throws me off.

You: Ah, got it. So the tidying I do each night disorients you in the morning?

Roommate: Yes, exactly.

You: Thanks for explaining. To be honest, hearing that makes me feel disappointed because I thought I was doing us both a favor by cleaning up.

Roommate: I appreciate the effort. I know I can be messy. But still.

You: Let's try to figure this out together. I think we both don't want the apartment to get too messy, but we also don't want to disorient you in the mornings.

Roommate: Right.

You: I have a few ideas. For starters, what if you show me now which things you never want me to move?

Does this conversation sound too . . . mature to be real? True, it is an artificially constructed one. But, it *can* work this way! People may come into a conversation hard, but when you are soft, they soften as well. You simply need to remember to step back from the heat of the moment—and they will often quickly follow.

Along similar lines, if you know that someone is angry with you and is really going to chew you out: Another of Dale Carnegie's insights is that you can preempt their criticism with an apology. If you proactively and sincerely say that you're sorry, it will often take the wind out of their sails—and may even make them want to apologize to *you* when they see that you're being hard on yourself.

One time, I really screwed up. I was running a mental-health tech startup, and I landed a partnership to apply for a grant with a prestigious hospital (which was way out of our league). We worked together on the application for months, but when the due date finally came, my team submitted it a few minutes late. Unfortunately, the grant program made no exceptions—a few minutes late was as good as a few weeks late, and they would not accept our application.

I decided to call our partner and tell them what happened. I apologized, and accepted the blame—even though it was someone else on my team who was responsible for submitting the application, and even though our partner was frequently late in delivering their parts to us. But I was the leader, and ultimately it was my responsibility to make the application happen. They were extremely disappointed, to be sure—but, to my surprise, instead of ranting about my failures (and saying something like, "That's what we get for taking a risk and working with such a small company," which was my deep fear), they apologized to me for how slow they were throughout the process. They told me they liked working together, and they agreed to try again for the next grant cycle.[38]

When you disagree with someone

When someone disagrees with you and you get into a debate, what are you trying to accomplish? Typically, the answers people give are:

- To convince the other person
- To win the debate
- To look smart in front of others

Unfortunately, those outcomes rarely happen. In the same way that people react defensively to criticism, their defenses also flare up when their opinions are challenged—and many times so when those opinions are related to deeply held beliefs on topics like politics or religion.

38 ... which we eventually got rejected from. One more rejection for my treasure chest!

In his book *The Righteous Mind*, the social psychologist Jonathan Haidt likens our minds to a rider sitting on top of an elephant. The elephant is the intuitive, reactive part of our mind; the rider is our rational side. We all think it's the rider controlling the elephant, but in reality—based on scores of experiments—it's actually the elephant who's in control. The elephant charges forward ("I'm not wrong!") and then the rider, rather than critically examining that reaction to determine if it's correct, uses its reasoning faculties to *justify* the elephant's position. In other words: People think they are using logic in disagreements way more than they are; in reality, their logic is only in service of backing up their preexisting opinions.

Knowing that, why even bother engaging in a disagreement? Are they pointless?

I used to study (and teach) a concept called "constructive disagreements"—called so because not only are disagreements not pointless, but in fact they can be the most productive type of conversation. They are an opportunity for both you and the other person to learn something new.

For example: What do you see here?

A green dog, right?

Wrong! It's actually a dog that's green on one side and white on the other side:

You only had a view of one side of the dog. If you spoke with someone on the other side, they would have insisted it's white:

Neither of you would be correct. You would need to speak with each other, and understand each other's (literal) viewpoint, in order to glean a complete picture of the truth.

Does that mean that all viewpoints are created equal? That we should give just as much credence to idiots and extremists?

Of course not all viewpoints have equal merit. For example, someone with a close-up view of only the dog's toenail (paw-nail?) would have insisted that the picture is of a toenail; they would be way more off base than your view that it's a green dog. However, that person *still* has something to teach you—you could learn more about the details of that toenail.

Which means . . . yes, it is sometimes worth giving credence to idiots and extremists. Because how do you *know* that they are wrong? What if it's you who has only the close-up view of the toenail?

The only way to gain a more complete picture of the truth is to converse *especially* with people with whom you disagree. In order for you to benefit from that disagreement, you need a different purpose—not to convince, or to win, or to look smart—rather, to learn.

Just as disagreement flares up people's defenses, curiosity lowers them. The more questions you ask, the more people open up.

Here is a process you can follow:

1. Start with shared intent – "I want to understand your opinion."
2. Ask questions – For example: "Why do you believe that?" or "I'm curious what first convinced you of that?" or "What else do you think people who disagree with you are missing?"
3. Repeat it back – They should be able to say that you've articulated their own viewpoint better than they could have.
4. Share assertively – Now you can state your own viewpoint, in a straightforward way, with no presumption of changing their mind.

If this sounds familiar, that's because it is! It's basically a mash-up of the framework for "when someone else needs something from you" (empathetic listening) plus "when you need something from someone else" (assertiveness). Navigating a disagreement is essentially the same as understanding someone else's needs (opinions), then sharing your own.

One final question: Is there really no hope for convincing someone else that you are right? It *is* possible, but don't expect it to happen during the course of one conversation. (How often have you really changed your mind about a deeply-held belief during the course of one conversation?) Think of it like planting a seed. The new idea you share—if the other person is really listening—can take root in the garden of their mind. Over time, they may hear or read more viewpoints that support it, and it will slowly get watered. It may eventually grow into a full plant (a belief), or it may not.

But in order to plant a seed in their garden, you need to be equally open to having one planted in yours.

SUMMARY

- Rather than being passive or aggressive or passive-aggressive, be assertive; you have the right to share your needs, and others have the right to choose to accommodate or ignore them.
- If you want to help someone improve, use positive reinforcement rather than criticism, and start by showing you are on the same team.
- When someone needs something from you or has feedback for you, utilize empathetic listening: Acknowledge their emotions, repeat back their concern, share your own emotions, then problem-solve.
- Disagreements can be incredibly constructive, but only if you approach them with curiosity; their purpose is to learn about other viewpoints, and maybe plant a seed of your own.

Homework

Seek out a disagreement! Find someone who has a different opinion on a strong belief (like politics or religion) and use the above techniques to learn more about it.

Extra credit: Identify one thing someone has been doing that's been bothering you, but you've been holding back on saying anything about it. Make your request to them assertively.

Skill #10

FIND FRIENDS (AND LOVE)

Unlike most of the other topics in this book, friendships and romantic love are quite subjective. My goal, as always, is not to tell you how to live—it's to help you figure out what you want, and how to get it. I'll do so by exposing pervasive myths, sharing personal examples, and offering frameworks (ways to think about complex questions).

The peerless post-college world

Shortly after graduating college, two harsh realities about friendship became clear:

1. Friendships no longer happen automatically – Growing up, you were surrounded by peers at school eight hours or more each day; in college, you were living in a mini city inhabited almost exclusively by peers for four or more years. You collided with each other over and over, not only in class but also while walking, over meals, and during activities. In the non-school world, you don't have a peer group. You don't have people whom you will keep seeing automatically, if you don't make an intentional effort (other than some coworkers, assuming you don't work remotely).

2. You don't have much time to spend with friends – Jonathan is one of my two best friends, and we were inseparable throughout high school. We still make an effort to see each other often as adults, but now that we live in different cities, "often" means once or twice per month. We recently calculated that we probably spent more hours together in high school than we will in the entire rest of our lives.

I hope this doesn't sound too bleak. Post-college life does not have to be lonely—it's just that it takes deliberate effort to be social. Unless you are naturally highly extroverted, friendships will likely no longer "happen" to you; you'll have to seek them out and develop them.

The work of friendships

These steps take effort:

1. Meeting new people – For some, this is fun; they like parties or trying out new experiences. But for many, those things can feel like chores. If that's you, it's okay—you can approach it as work, but work worth doing. In order to maximize your chances of meeting people you click with, there's no substitute for meeting *more* people. Going to parties and events or joining clubs gives you a lot of bang for your buck (time).

2. Following up – When you do click with someone, it's improbable that you'll naturally bump into them again like you could if you were walking around campus. Instead, you need to be the one to follow up and plan your next hangout (if you wait for them to be the one to do it, you may be waiting forever).

3. Keeping in touch – With some old friends, you outgrow them over time; with others, they become dearer over the time. For the latter category, treat them as more precious than your most precious objects—the history and intimacy you have can never be replaced. I find rituals to be really helpful; if you make a set, recurring time to send a text or call someone, it's more likely to happen.

I also think it's not irrational to be generous with good friends and make sacrifices for them, as you would with family members. And, just as you may prioritize family in other aspects of your life (such as choosing where to live), I don't think it's crazy to do so for the friends who matter most to you.

I started considering this in the context of long-distance friendships. I noticed they had a lot of the same pitfalls as long-distance relationships: When you do see each other, you spend almost all your time catching up on what you've missed in each other's lives, plus there's extra pressure to feel like you're having fun during your time together (because you have so little of it). Whereas when you see someone almost every day, you are a part of each other's lives; the daily ups and downs get shared as they happen.

If it sounds like a lot of these principles can apply to love and dating, that's because they can . . .

A personal story (perhaps applicable to a later life stage) – My other best friend, Daniel, married my wife's best friend, Julie (their first kiss was at our engagement party). Now they, like us, have little kids. We long harbored a dream of living side by side in neighboring houses, sharing meals and movie nights and effectively raising our children together. We tried to make it work multiple times, but we were always thwarted by reality: Daniel was tied to a specific location with his job and he wanted to be within short commuting distance, while our priority was being closer to the ideal school for our kids. The housing-market conditions made it difficult to find one house we liked, let alone the chances of two side by side happening to come up for sale at the same time, within our respective budgets.

Years passed. Then, in what felt like an act of fate, I happened to find out about a new townhome development a few days before the homes went on sale. Daniel and Julie visited the model home and told us they were considering it. I flew down the next day (for one day only—quite stressful!) and after walking through it, had one hour to decide if we wanted to buy it. What Charlotte and I agreed on was essentially: "We've been figuring out where to live and what kind of house to buy for years now. This is *not* the right house for us. It's too small, it has lots of staircases (not good for little kids), it's in a city that meets almost none of the criteria we had for an ideal place. And yet . . . all of those reasons pale in comparison to the opportunity to share a life with our best friends." So we bought the house next to theirs.

Of course, going all in may not be the right move for everyone—and you have to truly, deeply trust your friends to make it worth these sacrifices. I just think that, as we learned in skill #1, you can start by determining what's most important in your life, then designing everything else around those criteria.

More dimensions

The first few weeks that Charlotte and I dated were euphoric. We hung out every day and had so much fun getting to know each other better. Which is why our first argument hit me so hard. Walking back to my college dorm room afterward, I remember thinking, "This hurts so much. Dating isn't supposed to be painful; it's supposed to be fun."

To some extent, that's true; if someone brings you more heartache than joy, you probably aren't a good match. But otherwise, my thought was an immature way to view relationships.

Deep relationships—the kind you have with your spouse and your children—are not pure bliss, nor should they be. Deep relationships add new dimensions to your life. Each dimension can bring you more joy, more sadness, more love, more frustration. The purpose of adding more dimensions is not to bring you more moment-to-moment happiness (although there is certainly plenty of that), it's to bring you LTF (long-term fulfillment).

In doing so, you are diversifying your sources of meaning in life. If the only deep relationship you have is your relationship with work, then whenever you have a bad day at work, you've had a bad day, period. But if you come home to a partner you care about, or children, you can have a day that was "bad at work, but good at home" (or vice versa). Just as we learned in skill #6, if you don't put all your eggs in one basket, there's less risk that one bad investment ruins your entire life.

Knowing what we want from love is actually quite difficult, because we've unconsciously assimilated so much about love from growing up—from our parents' relationship, from books and songs, from our peer group. Some of those ideas are *so true* and some of them are *so false*. In particular . . .

Myths about romantic love

I love Disney movies, and as I grew up I began to love romantic comedies of all stripes as well—ranging from sappy to raunchy to indie. But most of what these movies convey about love is completely false. (I still think they're great entertainment, as long as you keep in mind that they're just as make-believe as superhero movies.)

Here are the top three myths:

1. "If you're attracted to other people, there's something wrong with your relationship."

The myth: When you're in a relationship, you won't be attracted to other people. If you are—and if you fantasize about what your life would be like if you were single, or with someone different—then you must be in a bad relationship.

The reality: You have zero control over whom you're attracted to. You also have little control over dreams and daydreams. It's natural to be attracted to people you find attractive, and it's natural to fantasize. Humans are born with a biological sex drive and we cannot magically shut off our subconscious, dreams, and daydreams as soon as we are in a monogamous relationship.

The solution: As we learned in skill #4, you have no control over your automatic thoughts; but you do have control over your revised thoughts. For example, you can revise your automatic thought from "I want to have sex with that person" to "Actually, I don't want to have sex with that person because I don't want to hurt my partner."

2. "Your ideal partner will fulfill all of your needs."

The myth: When you find your soul mate, they alone will be capable of making you happy. You won't need anything or anyone else except them.

The reality: No one has the exact same interests as you; that doesn't mean you can't be together. I love novels, but Charlotte reads only nonfiction, and talking about fiction puts her to sleep. So I started a writing workshop with my friends who also like reading and writing, and we met once every two weeks. Charlotte and I still fulfill so many of each other's needs; just not *all* of them.

The solution: Continue to spend time with your friends and family, and engage in your own hobbies. And by the same principle, if your partner spends time alone or with other people, it doesn't say anything about your ability to make them happy.

3. "Your partner should give up everything for you."

The myth: Your partner will sacrifice their career, friends, and life passions in order to make you happy. The more they sacrifice, the more they love you. By the same token, you should be willing to sacrifice everything for your partner.

The reality: Sometimes sacrifice is necessary to keep a relationship going, and sometimes it isn't. If no sacrifices are necessary, it doesn't mean your partner loves you any less. If sacrifices *are* necessary, it's usually not an all-or-nothing choice between love and career. You can prioritize the relationship and still make the best possible career decision within that constraint.

The solution: Even if your relationship constrains your time or geography, it provides enormous advantages. Your partner provides the support that is crucial to keep persisting during tough times, and they can push you to succeed more than you would push yourself. When my wife was studying biology for her medical-school entrance exams, we liked to say, "I'm a catalyst to your dreams, not an inhibitor."

Once you have overcome these and other myths, how do you go about finding the ideal partner? The first step is to recognize . . .

Dating is not something that happens to you, it's something you do

Another common myth is that you'll lock eyes with someone from across a crowded room, or serendipity will guarantee you will be in the same place at the same time. If it was "meant to be," it will be.

That does happen sometimes—to people who are extremely lucky. But banking on that happening is like banking on making all of your money by winning the lottery. Instead, as with making new friends, you can take certain steps to proactively maximize your chances of meeting your ideal partner . . .

But before we get into those steps, I want to take a moment to be real with you. I was heavily considering cutting this section from the book. I was cautioned by multiple friends and editors that it may land poorly, especially with readers in their twenties: "people that age aren't thinking about marriage nowadays"; "it feels so far away for them"; "it's not a priority for them." All of that may be true—which is why I ultimately decided it was *especially* important to share these lessons. Every person I know in their thirties who is single has told me that the dating pool was much better in their twenties, and they wish they had taken dating more seriously. Suddenly, it seems to them that all the best catches have been taken, and all their friends who previously had time for them are now consumed with raising children, and they are left alone, the last one standing, holding the bag, wondering how everyone disappeared so quickly.

If you remain skeptical, that is fine. If you think that you never want to marry—doubly so! You should decide for yourself what's important, and not make a life choice simply because it's what most people do. But if you suspect that you *one day* want to find a life partner, pretend that day is *today*. Because it may take one year to find that person, or it may take twenty years. I felt a deep need to write about this so that you don't end up like one of my many friends who is lonely and wishes they dated more seriously while it was easier to do so. I hope that, by now, I've built enough trust with you that you'll at least humor me on this point and consider:

1. Changing your mindset about dating – As I mentioned, I naively thought dating was supposed to be pure fun. But really, dating is like a massive treasure hunt: The prize (your ideal partner) is hiding somewhere, and you need to find it. It's normal for there to be obstacles and detours along the way. Going to parties or on blind dates may not sound intrinsically fun to you, and there are plenty of times you just don't feel like it, but sometimes you need to get through the less fun experiences to find the treasure.

If finding someone to share your life with is important to you, then this treasure hunt is *the most important thing you are doing*. In many cases, it's worth spending as much time on as you spend on your job—and approaching it with the same amount of energy and proactivity.

2. Broadening the search – Your ideal partner could be hiding anywhere. What will help you turn over the most stones? Not relying only on yourself—get the word out there! You can outsource the search to all of your friends. No need to be coy about it; tell all of them, "I'm looking for my ideal partner, and I need your help to find them." Most people who care about you want to help you.

Another great way of broadening the search is to use apps and websites that have millions of people on them. Many people have an aversion to apps and online dating—it feels too artificial, or they've been burned by it in the past. So, instead of viewing it as online dating, you can view it as online *meeting*. You're taking advantage of a database or an algorithm to find someone you wouldn't have otherwise met, and once you've met them, the entire process of dating them can take place IRL.

3. Sketching out your ideal partner – If you want your friends to be as helpful as possible, tell them exactly what you're looking for. Give them a list of criteria—the more details and examples, the better. Some categories you may want to include:

- Values – What is important to them in life? What (if any) religion are they and/or what morals do they hold themselves accountable to?
- Personality – How do they act around others? What is their sense of humor?

- Passions and interests – How do they like to spend their time? What sparks their curiosity?
- Physical appearance – What characteristics and features turn you on? For many people, this can be a wide variety. Share plenty of (realistic) pictures as examples of whom you find attractive. (I know this may seem awkward, but it's less awkward than showing up to a date set up by a friend and realizing you aren't attracted to the person at all.)

One criterion that I think gets woefully underrated: Is this a *happy* person? If you end up committed to them, so much of your happiness will depend upon their happiness. If they are incapable of being pleased—or, more specifically, if you are not capable of pleasing them (because all your love and efforts are not enough to fill them up)—you will likely end up unhappy as well. It may be hard to fully determine this in the early stages of dating, but there are some basic traits you can look for: optimism and positivity.

Then, once you've constructed the perfect partner on paper, retitle it "The 50% List." That's because your ideal partner—your true soul mate!—will probably check off 50% of this list, maximum. They will be a whole person, someone who defies your current imagination; they will have more flaws than you can imagine, and more hidden strengths and beautiful traits than you can imagine.

If you don't create a list at all, you'll be hunting for treasure by fumbling around in the dark; on the other hand, if you adamantly stick to 100% of your criteria, you won't even realize when you've found it.

4. Improving yourself – So far, we have covered only half the equation. What guarantees that, when you've decided you want to be with someone, they'll want to be with *you*? Nothing. But you can maximize your chances by working on yourself. A former student of mine came up with this brilliant question: "How can I become the kind of person who my ideal partner would want to be with?" Cultivate in yourself the kind of qualities you want in a future partner.

Per the third point, this search is even more difficult than a treasure hunt because it's not at all clear when it's over. How do you know if you're holding a piece of real gold versus a fake replica?

When to commit

Personally, I am a big fan of marriage. I think it's the right choice for many (though not all) people. However, I also believe that most people end up getting married *for the wrong reasons*. Specifically:

- Because they've been conditioned to believe it's the only viable path to living "happily ever after"
- Because it's what their friends are doing
- Because they have reached a certain age
- Because they have been dating someone for a certain amount of time
- Because their parents expect them to
- Because they want a perpetual source of loyalty and love in their life (they want someone to put into a box, to be opened whenever they feel like—if that's the case, I recommend getting a dog instead)

Alternatively, here are some of the more valid reasons to get married:

- No more evaluating – While your relationship is uncommitted, every new piece of information you learn about your partner is a point in favor or a point against them—each is helping you determine if you want to stay together. When you're committed, you can stop scoring your partner—you can learn about each other purely for the sake of getting to know each other better.
- Growing together – If you're still relatively young, you have plenty of learning and growing to do. Would you rather settle down with someone after you've ossified into a more permanent version of yourself (and they have done so

themselves), or grow together and shape each other into your adult selves?

- Have someone to bear witness to your life – The everyday things you do matter more when you know that you can tell them to someone who cares.
- A loneliness insurance policy – If you enjoy the company of others (or, more specifically, the company of the person you love most in the world) it can be comforting to know that you will have it every day. Also, nobody wants to die alone.

So how do you know when you're ready to make that commitment?

Imagine two piles of facts. One of them is the "reasons your partner is right for you" pile (good) and the other is the "reasons your partner is not right for you" pile (bad). If the former pile is larger by some satisfactory margin, then it's worth remaining in the relationship. Once you do, the "bad" pile becomes a list of things that are worth tolerating.

The problem is, there is a third pile: the "things you don't know" pile (unknown). You may know that you have fun on dates together, but you don't know if you share important values. Or you may know how your partner handles work stress, but you don't know how they handle family stress.

The unknown pile can be scary: There might be something there that, once discovered, would be a dealbreaker—or, at the very least, would make the bad pile too much larger than the good pile. You're constantly uncovering what's in that pile (learning new things about each other), but you will never uncover *everything*.

At some point, though, the good pile may grow so large that it's bigger than the bad pile *plus* the unknown pile combined. So, even if every unknown turned out to be something bad, the bad pile would still be smaller than the good pile.

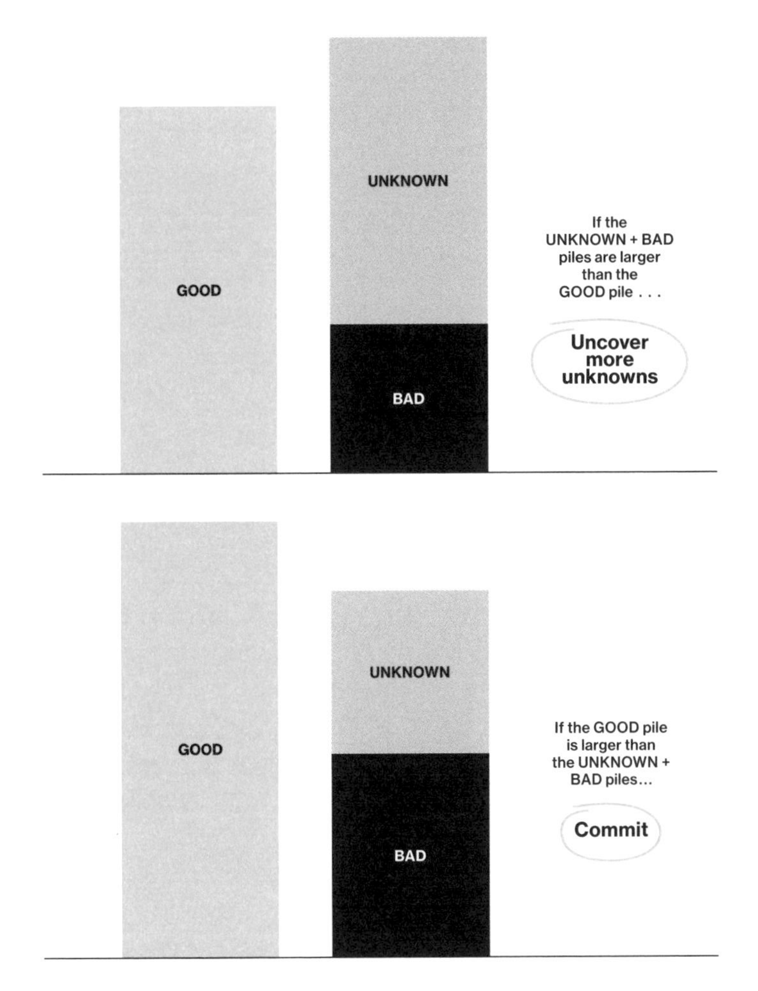

In other words, at some point you know enough things about your partner to know that your relationship is good enough—such that any as-of-yet-to-be-discovered flaw is something that is worth working through, rather than worth splitting up over (within reason, of course; being an axe murderer is probably a dealbreaker).

At that point, you can make this commitment to yourself and to your partner: "No matter what else we learn about each other, we will work through it together, because the good that we have is worth preserving."

Obviously, you can never be *totally* sure. That's another pervasive myth about love: "When you're in the right relationship, you won't have any doubts. You'll know with absolute certainty that this is the partner for you." In reality, no one is ever completely certain about anything. Even if you find the best possible partner for yourself, it's still unavoidable to be asking yourself questions like, "What if this very minor disagreement ends up becoming a major problem in our relationship?" or "What if they're not *really* the person I think they are?" or "What if we both change significantly; what if we fall out of love?" If you wait until your brain isn't floating any of these questions anymore, you'll be waiting forever.

On my wedding day, one of my groomsmen—who was considering proposing to his girlfriend—asked me, "How did you become 100% certain you want to marry Charlotte?" I told him the truth: "I'm not 100% sure. I'm more like 90% sure. But 90% is pretty high! To me, being okay with that remaining uncertainty is what love means."[39]

There's another myth we should deconstruct: "When you've committed to your partner, the quest is over and you will live happily ever after." Being happy in love forever *is* possible. However, once you've committed, the quest is not over—it's just beginning.

How to be a good partner

Most Disney movies and rom-coms end with the big wedding. My wedding was an incredible day—the best day of my life so far—but it's not like our relationship was frozen at that high point and sustained automatically in perpetuity. We had much to learn about how to build a good marriage.

Many people have an assumption that relationship skills (and sex) should come naturally—and if they don't, there's something wrong with your relationship. Of course, you need some baseline

39 Some days Charlotte finds my mathematical approach to love to be romantic. Some days she does not!

level of compatibility; but as with anything else, you can always improve it. In other words, being good at relationships is a skill that can be learned.

Of course, there is much that can be said here—what Charlotte and I have learned could be an entire book of its own; and what we have *not* yet learned could probably fill many more books. To start you on your journey, I'll tee up three main ways to become a better partner:

1. Treat them the way they like to be treated – This is not a platitude; everyone likes to be treated differently. There are many differences between you and your partner that may cause well-intentioned gestures to backfire. If your partner bakes you a birthday cake, you may find it incredibly sweet and feel touched; if you bake your partner a birthday cake, they may be disappointed that you've subjected them to your amateur baking skills on their special day instead of buying a nice cake from a store.[40]

The author Gary Chapman identified five "love languages," which are ways in which people express their love and feel loved. They are:

- Words of affirmation – saying loving things, giving encouragement and praise
- Physical touch – nonverbal displays of affection like hugging, kissing, holding hands
- Gifts – physical gifts as well as experiential gifts like going out or taking vacations
- Quality time – spending time focused on each other
- Acts of service – doing favors or "donating" your time (like doing their chores for them)

40 Another common difference: "In order to have sex, women need to feel loved; but in order for men to feel loved, they need to have sex" (attributed to the author David Mitchell).

As you probably noticed while reading this, different people are wont to express their love using different love languages. For example, when you want to make your partner feel loved, you may start planning a surprise date; when they want to make you feel loved, their go-to might be writing you a long handwritten card. Similarly, different people feel loved in different ways—for you, spending quality time may be the epitome of receiving affection; but your partner may not feel loved unless you tackle some of their chores each week.

You and your partner can go through this list one at a time and answer two questions: "How do I most like to express my love?" and "How do I most like to receive love?" Then, going forward, you can make an effort to express your love using the language(s) your partner most cares about—as well as appreciate when your partner expresses their love to you in their own way, even if it doesn't happen to be in your favorite language.

2. Communicate generously – Everything we learned about conversations in the last chapter applies here as well.

One additional tidbit: Assume positive intent. If your partner says something that hurts you, assume they didn't mean to hurt you; if they say something unhelpful, assume they were trying to help you. Often, these miscommunications happen when someone is not at their best—when they are tired or overwhelmed—in other words, when they *most* need your support.

3. Accept them for who they are, not who you want them to be – Charlotte will be the first to tell you that I have extremely high standards. From my employees, from my children, and especially from her, I expect amazing things. How do we resolve this paradox: Accept someone for who they are, *and* expect the best from them?

The key is the difference between wanting someone to change *in order to* love them, versus wanting someone to change *because* you love them. If you expect someone to change as a precondition to loving them, you are probably not with the right person. By contrast, when you deeply love someone, you see the best in them, and thus the better person they're capable of being.

SUMMARY

- Friendship will no longer just happen to you; you must invest effort into finding friends, following up, and keeping in touch with them.
- Most of what you've internalized about love from pop culture is wrong; you need to develop your own definition of love and a good relationship.
- Dating is a big treasure hunt that requires being proactive; you can broaden your search by using apps and by telling your friends that you want to be set up (and what kind of person you want to be set up with).
- Although many people get married for the wrong reasons, commitment has multiple intrinsic benefits; the time to commit is when the "good" pile has grown large enough that anything bad you uncover in the "unknown" pile will be worth working through rather than splitting up over.
- Making the commitment is the beginning of the story, not the end of it; in order to become a better partner, you can constantly work on treating your partner how they want to be treated (their preferred love languages), communicating generously (assume positive intent), and accepting them for who they are (while also expecting them to grow).

Homework

IF YOU ARE SINGLE... Ask someone out on a date.

One stipulation: Make it clear that you are asking for a date, not a hangout (or a hookup). You can use this as an opportunity to act on a crush you have, whether it's someone you already know or someone you barely know. And if it helps at all, you can tell them that you're doing it for this assignment.

Hopefully they'll say yes, and you have the date, and you end up having found the ideal partner (we can dream!). But if they decline, it can't hurt to have a backup plan... So, in addition, your second assignment is: Ask your friends to set you up. Create "The 50% List" and share it with them, telling them you are serious about finding your ideal partner and you need their help to make it happen.

IF YOU ARE IN A RELATIONSHIP... Determine how large your good, bad, and unknown piles currently are. If the good pile is not yet large enough to commit, think of one experiment you can do to uncover a big "unknown." Have you been on an intense trip together? Have you lived in the same space? Have you met each other's family? Discuss it with your partner and propose this next step.

IF THE BAD PILE IS TOO LARGE, AND YOU'RE REALIZING NO AMOUNT OF GOOD THINGS THAT MAY BE HIDING IN THE UNKNOWN PILE CAN MAKE UP FOR IT... It's probably time to break up. If you make that determination, then your assignment is: End the relationship. Once you've determined your relationship is going nowhere, don't waste more time on it—you have a lot more treasure hunting to embark on! Do it face-to-face (assuming you've been dating long enough, it's a courtesy you would probably appreciate yourself).

I know a lot of this may feel unconventional, or overly assertive. But I hope you're open to trying it. You're an adult—now is the time to take responsibility for your own love life.

Extra credit: Write your own definitions of love (and revise them over the years).

Skill #11

EVOLVE WITH YOUR PARENTS

The first decision I made that really upset my parents was when I was twenty-four years old. Sure, I had made plenty of choices they disagreed with here and there, but overall they probably believed that the trajectory of my life would be in line with what they had expected from me.

On my commute home from work, I called to tell them that I wasn't going to business school. I had already been accepted—and paid the deposit—but decided to drop out a few weeks before the semester started.

"It's not too late!" my mother pleaded. "If you call them and tell them that it was a mistake, and you're really sorry, they may still let you back in . . ."

This was the culmination of months of deliberation, despite campaigning from my family. My parents believed that business school was the best move for my career, rather than doing what I was planning to do—become an entrepreneur. (More to come in skill #13 about making big career decisions.)

Part of their reasoning likely came from my grandparents, who told me, "Jobs come and go, but the only thing you can really take with you is your degree." They were referring to their own parents' and grandparents' experience, having needed to uproot their lives to escape anti-Semitic persecution. It was as if this centuries-long trauma—of needing to be ready to pick up and leave, on a moment's notice, and start over somewhere entirely new (where only their educational pedigree would be valued)—had been passed down from generation to generation. And it probably served most of my ancestors well, given their life circumstances. But I was (thankfully!) in different circumstances: My parents had generously uprooted *their* lives to move to the United States so that they could raise a family in the freest, safest country in the world. It's highly unlikely that in my lifetime I will need to flee the United States to escape persecution and start over in a new country.

My parents are wise and I always valued their advice. This was the first time I finally realized that I may know more about what was best for me than they did.

The shifting Venn diagram

Most parents want what is best for their child in the long term. When you were little, and you and they disagreed about what was best for you, they were probably right and you were wrong. As a three-year-old, you may have wanted to eat sweets all day, and they knew—given that their brains were more developed than yours, and they had more experience than you—that doing so would lead to misery. As a ten-year-old, you may have wanted to skip school every day, but they knew that learning was important. And so on. Thus, in the Venn diagram of "what is best for you," there was way more overlap with "what your parents thought" than with "what you thought":

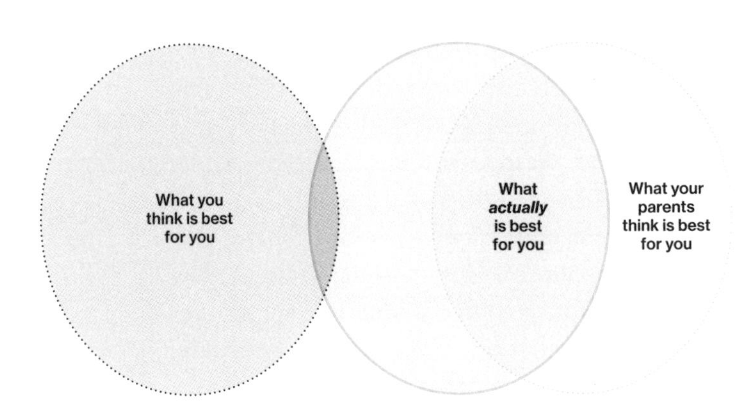

By the time you are twentysomething, your brain is more developed. You have more life experience. And your parents' life experience may have become less relevant, because the world has changed. Most critically, *you know yourself better than they do*. You've had time to experiment in life and learn about your own ideals and behavior. Presumably, you have spent time living away from home; your parents are no longer with you every day, so they are less privy to all the ways you've changed. The Venn diagram has shifted, and will probably continue to shift:

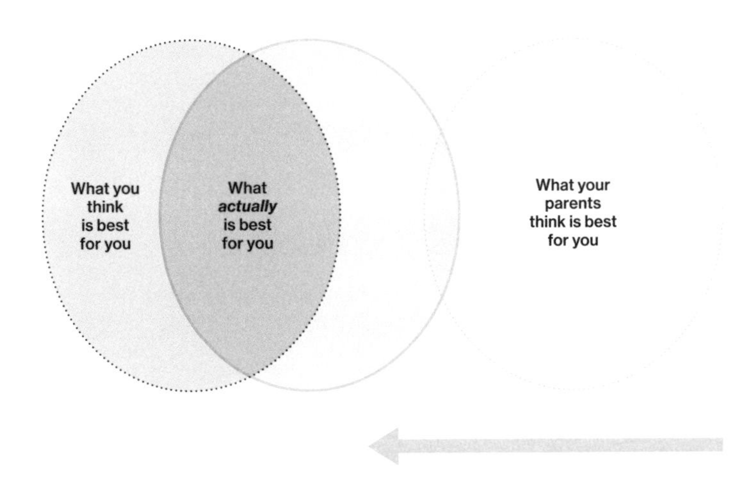

Of course, this doesn't mean you are right all the time! It means that now it is up to you to listen to your parents' advice carefully and discern, rather than doing what they want by default.

It's not always clear—to your parents, or to you—where you are along this Venn diagram migration. People change slowly, and it's hard to notice until they have become quite different. In many cases, people become *more themselves* as they get older; the more time they have spent away from their parents, the less they are subconsciously adapting their personality to be in line with what their parents expect. A passage from the end of the book *Middlesex*, by Jeffrey Eugenides, captures this perfectly:[41]

> "Don't you think it would have been easier just to stay the way you were?"
>
> I lifted my face and looked into my mother's eyes. And I told her: "This is the way I was."

One of the hardest (and in my opinion, one of the most important) things about being a parent is noticing the changes in your children, and not only adapting to them, but even pushing them along in their journey to become more like themselves.

What do you owe?

Navigating this transition is difficult. Understandably so—the entire dynamic of your relationship with your parents has now shifted! They are no longer there to steer your ship; you are steering your own ship.

Many parents react in extreme ways when this realization finally hits them. My friends and I call this the "Post-Wedding Parents' Freak-Out" (PWPFO), because in our experience it often

41 This particular quote is about a character who is born intersex and changes sexes, but as a metaphor I think it applies broadly.

happens when their child gets married. They realize that now it is someone else, not they, who is the primary influence in their child's life.

A brilliant movie from the 1960s, *Guess Who's Coming to Dinner*, is all about the PWPFO. A white woman visits her parents with her new fiancé, a black doctor named John. Despite the parents not being overtly racist, they are clearly uncomfortable with her decision, primarily citing that the country has not fully accepted interracial marriage and thus their union will make their lives more difficult.[42] Toward the end of the film, John's parents visit, and likewise disapprove of the marriage. John's father talks about how hard he worked (walking "75,000 miles" as a mailman) and how much John's mother sacrificed to get him through school so that he could have a better life. Finally, in an epic monologue, John (played by Sidney Poitier) pushes back on his father. Here are some of the highlights:

> *You don't even know what I am, Dad. You don't know who I am. You don't know how I feel, what I think.* Children change, and eventually know themselves better than their parents.

> *You are thirty years older than I am. You and your whole lousy generation believe the way it was for you is the way it's got to be. And not until your whole generation has lain down and died will the dead weight of you be off our backs!* Pretty harsh, but perhaps true. It echoes the earlier point about parents' experiences becoming less relevant as they age because the world is changing.

---

42 Fun fact: In the movie, the couple meets at the University of Hawaii, and John says that his fiancée is optimistic about their future; she "feels that all of our children will be president of the United States." In real life, also in the 1960s, a white woman and black man met at the University of Hawaii, got married, and had a child . . . who did become president of the United States (Barack Obama).

Let me tell you something: I owe you nothing. If you carried that [mail]bag a million miles, you did what you were supposed to do. Because you brought me into this world, and from that day you owed me everything you could ever do for me—like I will owe my son . . . But you don't own me. In other words: Having a child was their choice. Now, they must let him make his own choices.

Dad . . . Dad. You're my father. I'm your son. I love you. I always have, and I always will. The intense monologue ends on a sweet note (and with the music swelling).

When the students in my Adulting 101 class discussed the film, John's third point raised strong feelings. Was sacrificing so much for John what his parents were *supposed* to do? Did they owe John everything they could ever do for him, simply by virtue of him being their child? Those are great questions for prospective parents to grapple with. But as (current) adult children, the students mostly wanted to answer the question: What do we owe our parents?

Before I share what emerged from that discussion, first think about it for yourself.

What do you owe your parents?

Here are the main answers the students shared:

- Love
- Gratitude
- Respect
- *Sometimes*: Financial support (pay it backward, since they supported me)
- *Sometimes*: Having children of my own (pay it forward, since they had me)

Of course, these are highly personal questions with answers that vary by background and culture. There is no one-size-fits-all model. But what I found most interesting was the answer to the question "What do you *not* owe your parents?" There was one pretty much unanimous answer:

- To always do what they want

It may seem like a contradiction. Wouldn't respecting your parents necessitate heeding their advice? Wouldn't being grateful to them necessitate not going against their wishes? Not so! You can respect your parents by asking for—and listening carefully to, and seriously considering—their advice. But you don't have to follow it. Similarly, John from *Guess Who's Coming to Dinner*, in the final words of his monologue, is able to express gratitude—where being grateful does *not* equal having to do exactly what his father wants.

Most people's parents want them to be happy in the long term (to attain LTF). If that's the case, then you owe it not only to yourself but *also to them* to occasionally decide against their wishes, given the shifting Venn diagram.

An overdue conversation

These changing dynamics can lead to tensions that continue to rise beneath the surface, until they are brought to light. With your romantic partner, when the parameters of your relationship change, it can become necessary to have a "define the relationship" (DTR) conversation; so, why not with your parents as well?

For this chapter's homework, I will ask you to have a DTR with your living parent(s) or parental figure(s). Here is an agenda for the conversation that has worked well for my students in the past:

- Define the relationship as it currently is
  - How often do you see each other?
  - How often do you communicate?

— What is your financial dependency situation?

- How *they* would like the relationship to be
  — How often should you see each other?
  — How often should you communicate?
  — How dependent should you be financially?

- How *you* would like the relationship to be
  — How often should you see each other?
  — How often should you communicate?
  — How dependent should you be financially?[43]

- Gain deeper understanding
  — What is one thing you wish they knew about you?
  — What is one thing you wish you knew about them?

Here are some tips for maximizing the chances that it goes well:

- Don't feel pressure to cover *everything* in one conversation. The purpose is simply to lay the groundwork for a more open, clearer relationship going forward. Focus on understanding their views, and helping them understand yours.
- Set up the conversation intentionally: Tell your parents that you want to have it, and why. (If it helps, you can tell them that this book is forcing you to!) Pick a time and location that works well for all of you—somewhere that puts you all at ease, whether that's in your parents' living room or at their favorite restaurant.

43 If you rely on your parents for income, it may be worth asking yourself whether it remains worthwhile. If they are paying an essential expense, such as rent that you could not afford on your own, perhaps you'll want to maintain the status quo; but if you are on their family phone plan while being otherwise independent, you may want to cut the cord entirely, because even a small amount of money can have invisible strings attached to it.

- Beforehand, think of two or three things that you appreciate about the way they raised you. Start by sharing those.
- Use the frameworks for effective communication from skill #9, in particular, empathetic listening (first acknowledge, then repeat, then share) and assertiveness—you can state your desire for how you want your relationship to be without holding back, and also without expecting that they should accommodate those desires just because you are their child.
- When talking about what you would like the relationship to be going forward, focus mostly on things that are good that you want to continue (or have more of). Only pick one important thing that you want to change.

Of course, this conversation may at first feel awkward. It's probably worth pushing through some awkwardness in order to gain deeper intimacy with your parents—especially before any strife builds up past its boiling point.

Having kids

I alluded earlier to prospective parents. When going deep into these topics with your parents, it's natural to think about how you would like to do things differently when you have children of your own. Which raises the obvious questions: *Do* you want to have children of your own? And if so, when?

As with marriage, I personally worry that many people have children for the wrong reasons:

- Because it is expected of them
- Because they want their children to be successful in their career so that they can feel successful
- Because they want to relive their own life, but without making the same mistakes

- Because they are lonely and want someone to love
- Because they are lonely and want someone to love them

I think these are wrong reasons because each of them puts expectations on your children. They will be born into the world with a purpose that is *not* solely to achieve their own LTF. They will be born into a kind of indentured servitude—in return for having birthed them, they must now "repay" you by becoming successful, or by giving you attention, and so forth. To me, it doesn't seem fair to give birth to indentured servants.

Of course, these beliefs are on a spectrum. It's perfectly natural to really want your child to love you, or to feel a strong desire to have a family so you can share your love, or even to want your child to become successful so that you can brag about them. However, choosing to have them for one of those purposes *entirely* is what places unfair expectations on them.

So, what are the *right* reasons to have children? You must determine those for yourself! Recalling the Google Doc metaphor from skill #1, think about all your ingrained beliefs about having kids, identify where those beliefs actually came from, and which ones you still agree with. You can start exploring further by seeking out different perspectives, reflecting deeply, and discussing it with your partner if you have one.

In case it's helpful, here is the list of reasons that my wife and I came up with:[44]

1. Existence – Most people are very glad they exist! If we decided that we couldn't have one (more) child, then that person wouldn't exist—and it feels like, "Sorry, we didn't have enough energy or money" is a paltry excuse to tell someone for why they never got to exist.

44 To be fully transparent, we came up with most of these *after* having our first child. That event compelled us to think more deeply about whether or not we wanted to have more. I *think* our reasons for having our first were also decent ones—let's hope he doesn't grow up to be the one child of ours who feels like an indentured servant!

2. Net utility – We think that the average human has, on average, a good life (according to their own perceptions). Thus, if you are philosophically utilitarian—if you measure goodness as the sum of positive conscious experience minus negative conscious experience—then more humans lead to more net positive utility in the world.

3. Team Judaism – We are Jewish and really want the Jewish religion and Jewish people to continue to exist. (As one of my high school teachers put it: Hitler killed six million of us; each child that we have is like giving a big middle finger to the Nazis.)

4. Team human – We are big fans of the human species. We want there to be more of us, and for our species to continue to exist. We are worried about recent data showing that population growth across the world is slowing. In many countries, it has even started to *decline* (see South Korea for a stark example). We want to play our part, however small, in contributing to the survival of the species.

5. Global well-being – Some people worry about overpopulation, or about the additional resources that more humans consume. However, in our research, we've found that a larger global population is positively correlated with higher well-being for the average human: As the world population has increased, so has average life expectancy, income, lower poverty, lower infant mortality, and many more improvements.

6. Innovation – There are certainly massive existential problems facing the human species. We believe that one of the best ways to solve them is through having children, because each child is a possible Albert Einstein or Jonas Salk—someone who can discover ideas or innovate solutions that eventually will solve these problems.

Depending on who you are, your optimal life path may be to have no children, or to have as many children as possible, or anywhere between those opposite ends of the spectrum.

I would be remiss if I didn't mention the harsh reality that biology imposes upon women in particular: There is a ticking time limit. With modern medicine and new technology, it can feel easier than ever to put off making this decision. Thankfully, women are able to have children in their forties, and IVF (in-vitro fertilization) and other fertility solutions are constantly improving. However, natural fertility declines with age, and the health risks associated with pregnancy—for both women and babies—increase with age. None of these technologies are miracle solutions (ask any couple who's been through IVF). Similarly, adoption can be a great option, but it is often quite challenging—ask any couple who has been through the process and they will tell you that it is long, emotionally difficult, expensive, and does not always result in a successful adoption.

My concern is not that you decide to have kids when you are older; that may be a perfectly good decision. My concern is that you *put off even deciding* until you are older. By that point, you may find that your options are woefully limited. If you are more on the "have many children" end of the spectrum, then the earlier you start, the more you can have[45]—and thus, dating seriously (as we learned last chapter) becomes even higher of a priority.

45 For my own family, this meant having kids while my wife was in medical school and during residency, when many of her peers were not yet having children. Unfortunately, the rate of infertility is particularly high among doctors and other professions that require many years of training.

SUMMARY

- As you get older, your parents begin to know you less well; the Venn diagram of "what is best for you" overlaps less with "what your parents think is best for you" and more with "what you think is best for you."
- It is possible to give your parents love, gratitude, and respect without needing to always make the life decisions that they want.
- Your relationship with your parents will likely evolve to the point that a "define the relationship" (DTR) conversation becomes crucial; the goal is to understand their wishes, share yours, and lay the groundwork for a more communicative relationship.
- Everyone must determine their own reasons to have (and not to have) children; because of the harsh reality of female biology, you cannot put off making this decision for too long.

Homework

Have that DTR conversation with your parents! See the tips earlier in the chapter on how to best set it up.

Extra credit: Write your own list of reasons to have (and not to have) children. Keep updating it over time.

IV.

Career Skills

Skill #12

ACE YOUR FIRST JOB

If, until now, your entire career has been full-time schooling, there has typically been only one metric of success: grades. It was mostly clear how to get good grades—demonstrate your knowledge or cleverness (on exams and papers). But once you graduate, with a few exceptions such as academia, none of your bosses will care how much you demonstrate your knowledge or cleverness. What they care about is how much work you get done and what results you achieve. It's a totally different game! And one that few people have been prepared for.

My own rude awakening came at the end of a two-week training at my first full-time job, which was in management consulting. We had to research and deliver a presentation about a hypothetical client. I was ready to impress; I had followed every instruction to a T. During the mock presentation, the partners at the firm, who were pretending to be my client, started interrupting with all kinds of questions and comments: "How would that projection change by region?" and "What if the sales team doesn't accept these recommendations?" and "We've been told this before, and we disagree."

It felt so obnoxious. Why wouldn't they just let me finish my (immaculate) presentation? As I soon learned, they were doing a pretty accurate impression of clients. Not because the clients were obnoxious; rather, because what clients wanted was to understand our research and to know how to put it into action. Being dazzled by a fancy presentation had nothing to do with it. They would poke and prod and ask as many questions as they needed. In the real world, there were no "instructions" on how to earn an A from a client—the only metric was whether we could help them achieve results.

Of course, there are many people on a team who are accountable to these results, and if you are new, then you are likely at the bottom of that hierarchy, so the grunt work gets pushed down to you. Entry-level jobs, no matter the industry, are often filled with work that is much less intellectual than you may have been promised. To correct some common marketing pitches from on-campus recruiters:

- *Work in consulting to "shape strategy for clients"* – You do arithmetic in spreadsheets and resize boxes in PowerPoint.
- *Work in publishing to "discover the next great American novel"* – You skim through the slush pile.
- *Work in a lab to "cure cancer"* – You pipette all day.

At its worst, I felt like I was doing work that a trained monkey could do. I had been educated for sixteen years . . . why was I spending my time doing monkey work? It was demoralizing.

I wish I had realized that, just like school, this was also a game, albeit one with rules that were much less obvious.[46] Instead of trying to prove—to myself and others—that it was too easy or that I was above it, I should have seen it as a new challenge. And the faster you

46 If "winning" the game of school (getting good grades) was not your thing, don't worry—work is quite different from school. Many people who didn't thrive at (or care much about) school really begin to thrive in the workplace.

can master that challenge, the faster you move out of that monkey work stage of your career.

Although the rules of the game vary from workplace to workplace, there is one metric that is universal . . .

Make your manager's life as easy as possible

It's often said that the most useful skill for any career is empathy. If you can put yourself in your customers' shoes, you can understand how to persuade them to buy; if you can put yourself in your patients' shoes, you can understand how to care for them. By that same principle, if you can put yourself in your manager's shoes, you can understand what they need from you.

Your manager has goals they are accountable for meeting. They have resources at their disposal (money, staff) that they need to allocate to best meet those goals. The more you can do for them, the more time they have to allocate to other projects. The more they can trust you to get things done properly without needing too much oversight, the more they can worry about other things.

Here are some principles you can use to make their life easier:

1. Act like the owner of every project that you touch – The moment you take on a new project, you are responsible for the outcome, not your manager. It isn't their job to follow up with you to make sure something is getting done (they should be able to assume that it is getting done); rather, it's your job to follow up with them when you need their input and help.

This is a reversal from the typical supervisor-supervisee relationship you're probably familiar with, in which someone just tells you exactly what to do. But no one wants to be micromanaged! And your manager won't have any need to micromanage you if you are "managing up"—if you take responsibility for making the goal happen, and use *them* for support and advice when you need it.

2. Proactively share bottlenecks – Whenever an unexpected problem arose that could impact my ability to finish a task on time, I was tempted to not tell my manager about it. "I should just try to fix it and get through it. If I tell them about the problem but then it ends up being all right, I've wasted some goodwill with them for nothing." Sometimes I got lucky and finished on time, but other times I missed the deadline, which caught my manager by surprise.

Most managers would much rather know about potential deadline issues *before* they impact you, even if they end up being surmountable. I feared they would see me as incompetent for flagging a problem that was solvable; but I've since learned that they would see me as *more* competent for foreseeing potential issues and being transparent.

3. Instead of "no," say "yes, if" – Nobody likes hearing "no." If your manager has a plan and they are relying on you to do something, hearing "no" throws a wrench in that plan and can cause a headache.

Sometimes, you might have legitimate reasons for saying no: You may think that what they want is not possible, or you may know that there aren't enough hours in the day to finish this new thing plus everything else that's on your plate. In that case, you can say "yes, if":

- "*Yes*, I can make ten more sales this week, *if* the copywriting team gives me that new content."
- "*Yes*, I can do this new task, *if* we're willing to reprioritize this other thing and push its deadline to next week."

That way, you're putting yourself and your manager on the same team: You both want to do the new thing they're asking for, and now you're figuring out together how to make that feasible.

4. Use the cardboard cutout test – It's rarely frowned upon to ask for help or input; at the same time, you don't want to waste your manager's time on things you could have easily figured out for yourself. So, pretend there's a cardboard cutout of them next to your desk. Whenever you're tempted to email or call your manager with a question, first ask the cardboard cutout. You may be surprised to find that, once you know your manager well enough, the cutout can answer your questions the majority of the time.

The same goes for when you're about to submit a work product. Pretend the cardboard cutout is reading it—what feedback would they have? You can implement that feedback now, before you send "vFINAL" to your real manager.

5. Have zero defects – "ZD" (Zero Defect) was an important principle at my consulting company, and I often failed miserably on it. I'd have occasional typos on slides or math mistakes in spreadsheets that I got in trouble for. To me, the fuss seemed disproportionate to the error—I got 99% of the thing right, so why did that little 1% matter? On an exam, a 99% would have been an A+! For better or worse, the company was committed to being perfect for our clients, and thus associates like myself had to be perfect as well. More generally, most managers feel that if they can't trust you on the little things, then they cannot trust you on the big things.

Even when I committed to being more ZD, I still couldn't catch certain typos. After rereading the same document several times, my eyes would glaze over. Eventually, I adopted these tactics, which helped tremendously:

- Take a long walk (outside), then come back to it with fresh eyes.
- Read it out loud, slowly.
- Print it (on real paper!) and read it that way.
- Use a text-to-voice program to hear it read out loud.
- Send it to a colleague and ask for their help (you can become proofreading buddies).

6. Mind the 80/20 rule – The "80/20 rule" is another helpful framework I learned from consulting.[47] Sometimes, 80% of the value is in 20% of the effort. In other words, you can spend two hours doing an A- job instead of ten hours doing an A+ job. Often, an A- job is all that's needed, and your manager would appreciate you saving your time to spend elsewhere.

Note that 80/20 and ZD can still be true at the same time: You can do an A- job while still making sure there are no errors that impact the validity or the readability of what you're submitting. That being said, you can always ask: "Do you want me to do the A- version, which will take about two hours, or the A+ version, which will take about ten hours?"

7. Just ask what your manager wants – I saved the simplest for last! The first time you meet with a new manager, ask them to share with you:

- What should everyone who works for you know about you?
- What are your pet peeves?
- For everyone who has worked for you successfully in the past, what made them successful?

There's another critical principle here, but it's so important that it deserves its own section . . .

Write for a CEO, not a professor

Almost everything you learned in school has made you a terrible writer. You've probably been trained to string out one idea into a lengthy essay; to use flowery language; to reference obscure

[47] Don't worry, I'm sparing you from the vast majority of the consulting frameworks. These are the most helpful ones, which I still remember ten years later.

terminology; to litter your pages with references and footnotes.[48] If you want to be a good writer of emails and memos in the workplace, you'll need to unlearn all of that.

The best advice I ever got about writing didn't come from a professor, or even a manager—it came from a fortune cookie:

Get to the point and keep it clear and simple.

I liked this fortune so much that I put it in the little picture slot of my wallet, so I see it each day. It reminds me to do the following when writing an email or memo:

1. Make the email as short as possible – Often, what seems like a complex thought in my head can really be reduced to a sentence or two. I like the "talk it out" method of trying to explain it to myself in my head more and more succinctly. You can even use a voice recorder to record all your thoughts, then try to type up an outline and rearrange it until it flows logically and concisely.

Yes, this is additional work. As the mathematician Blaise Pascal wrote: "I have only made this letter longer because I have not had the time to make it shorter."

2. Make the email as easy to read as possible – Don't be wordy. Only use acronyms if you're sure the recipient knows what they mean. Break up your long paragraphs; each paragraph should have only one main idea. Bullet points are your friend (lists are easier to digest than long text).

3. Use one call to action per email, and make it stand out – What do you want the recipient of your email to do? Make that "call to action" stand out by putting it at either the end or the beginning. I've noticed that if you have one request, the recipient will fulfill one request; if you have two requests, they will fulfill neither.

---

48 Sorry.

If you want, you can set your call to action in bold to make it clear what the purpose of the email is. (In some workplaces that is common practice; in others, it can be perceived as **aggressive**.)

I think one of my superpowers is writing great emails. I love to craft them—finding the perfect way to be comprehensive yet concise, striking the perfect tone. I could talk about emails for a long time (people at parties *love* me) . . .

I will spare you, but not before we do some practice examples together.

Practice 1.

How would you improve this email?

Subject: Deciding between two different graphic design options for the flyer

Dear Morgan,

I hope you are having a good week so far. I wanted to reach out with a question and see if you might be able to help me make a decision and provide final approval for this.

We received from the graphic designers two different templates that we can use for the flyer, which is due on Friday. You may recall that I already submitted my copy, which you have already approved. Now, we must decide which graphic template to use.

In terms of the options, I think A is immediately more appealing to the eye. The colors also match our other materials. I cannot see the font as well, however. Lastly, the image is bright; however, I do not think that depicting a crying monkey is the right message for this.

Looking toward option B, I am undecided. The colors are worse but the font is better. The picture of a smiling owl is nice. What do you think?

In summary, I am torn between options A and B. I will defer to you on this decision and will await your approval.

Sincerely,
Mel

Here's my edit:

Subject: [Approval requested] Graphic design for flyer

Morgan – **Can you please let me know by Friday if you approve the following decision?** If not, happy to defer to your judgment, but wanted to first provide my recommendation.

The graphic designers provided two options: A and B (attached).

I recommend B:
- More legible font
- Better image (smiling owl = happiness)
- One con: fewer bright colors

—Mel

I like including a tag in [brackets] in the subject line making it clear if you need input, or approval, or "FYI" (if you are just keeping the recipient in the loop). The email should start with the call to action, without a preamble. Also, you should always give your recommendation first! That makes it easier for your manager—they simply need to say "yes" or "no" (rather than deciding for you).

Practice 2.

How would you improve this email?

Subject: Proposal to all convene for a meeting sometime soon

Hey team,

I know there's been some back-and-forth about the status of the Pepsi client and everyone's involvement in that.

On the one side, we have the deadline next Tuesday that Amy, John, and Boris are all working toward. What is the status there? Are we on track? If not, we'll need to let Terry know so that she can plan accordingly.

On the other side, we have the interviews we are supposed to do after Tuesday. Do we want to divide and conquer? Or just delegate all of them to one person?

Lastly, the client meeting next Friday . . . Who is handling the logistics of getting there? Is there anything else we need to be considering?

Anyway, I know this is a lot. Perhaps we should all meet together to hash it out? Let me know if you agree, and if so you can feel free to share what times you are available.

Here's my edit:

Subject: Agenda for new meeting tomorrow (9/23)

Team – There's some confusion about the Pepsi client and I think we should meet to clear it up.

I've sent you all a calendar invite for a time tomorrow that appears to work for everyone's schedule.

Proposed agenda:
- Status of Tuesday deadline (goal: update Terry)
- Interviews task (goal: assign owners)
- Client meeting (goal: decide about logistics)

See, shorter is better! Although people often have way too many meetings and most of them are useless (in my humble opinion[49]), sometimes meetings are necessary to get everyone aligned. When that's the case, you can proactively schedule it by looking at the availability on everyone's calendars (to avoid the back-and-forth) and share the agenda in advance.

Once you've become a great writer, and mastered the other techniques to make your manager's life easier, it may beg the question . . . Do you actually *want* to please your manager? Do you care about acing your job, about winning this game?

---

49 And in the opinion of millions and millions of people the world over.

It depends. If you think that succeeding at this job will help you reach your goals, then commit to acing it. In other words, make a game out of the monkey work—one that motivates you to win—because you know that being promoted, or getting this credential on your resume, will help you build the career you want. But if you realize that succeeding at this job will *not* help you reach your goals—or if you have a toxic manager who is impossible to please—you may need to find a different job. It's certainly not quick or easy to do so, but once you realize you're not on the path that you want, the faster you realign it, the better.

The next chapter will focus on how to get a job, and more broadly how to build the career that you want. For now, we will cover one more topic relevant to your current job: How can *you* get the most out of it for yourself?

Own your professional development

There are many things a job can give you, the most obvious being your salary and benefits. But I think those are even less important than *developing yourself*. The more you learn and grow, the more successful you will be (and the more you can earn salary-wise in the long term).

In school, doing what was asked of you was (at least theoretically) aligned with you learning as much as possible. At work, you won't necessarily optimize for learning unless you make it a point to do so. I've found that most managers are open to supporting your growth as long as—like with everything else—you make it easy for them. So, as with every project you touch, treat your own professional development (PD) as a project that you own.

You can start by making a list of the skills you want to develop in the short term. Reflect back on your last week of work: What energized you? What did you feel particularly good at? What do you still want to work on?

Then, schedule a "PD chat" with your manager, ideally recurring every three weeks. Here is the agenda I like to use during my PD chats:

- Each project I am working on (listed in bullet points), with an excitement level for each (on a scale of one to ten) – to give your manager a sense of what type of work you prefer to do more or less of
- My PD goals from last time:
    - Which have I improved on
    - Which have I struggled with
- Your feedback for me
- My feedback for you

Feedback is critical! Unless you ask for it frequently, you may not get it.

Of course, hearing feedback can be difficult. I distinctly remember one PD chat in which the feedback I received made me struggle to hold back tears. Not because it was untrue; rather, because I knew it *was* true. Feedback is a mirror. It can be jarring to see what you look like—yet that is the only way to improve your own reflection. It may be painful, but the alternative is worse; if you don't learn how to improve, you will stagnate, becoming a Sisyphus pushing the boulder up the hill every day.

Even people who care about feedback sometimes unconsciously discourage others from sharing it—when they hear it, they seem to grow angry, or wilt. That disincentivizes the other person from sharing it next time. You can try this process:

1. When you hear the feedback, pause and take one deep breath. Don't think about whether or not it's true; just breathe.

2. Smile, look the other person in the eye, and say, "Thank you. It's really helpful for you to share that. I am going to think about it."
3. Later, when you're in a better mood, reflect on the feedback. Does it resonate? If you think it's not true (and that's not just your inner self-justifier talking!), you don't need to worry about it.
4. If you think it is true, show the other person that their feedback makes a meaningful difference—by acting on it. Draft a few next steps you can take. What are some things you can do now to start improving? Treat those things with as much urgency as your highest-priority work tasks.
5. The next time you speak with that person, thank them again for their feedback, and share the steps you've taken to improve. Ask them to hold you accountable to continuing to improve.

SUMMARY

- **Embrace the monkey work; acing your first job is a game, just like acing school was.**
- **Make your manager's life as easy as possible: Fully own every project you touch; don't be shy about sharing bottlenecks when they arise; instead of saying "no," say "yes, if."**
- **Unlearn everything school taught you about writing; remember the fortune cookie's sage advice: "Get to the point and keep it clear and simple."**
- **Own your professional development as you'd own any other project; in PD chats with your manager, proactively ask for feedback, then act on it.**

Homework

Write a straightforward, concise email to your manager expressing your desire to work on your professional development and request that you schedule recurring PD chats every three weeks (and share a draft agenda for the first one).

Extra credit: Look back at your recent email history at work for a time you said "no." Follow up with that person to offer a different solution ("yes, if").

Skill #13

LAUNCH YOUR CAREER

The good news is, now you know how to succeed in your first job. The bad news is, now you have two jobs: your day job, and the job of figuring out what in the world you want to do with your career.

A couple years into my first job as a management consultant, I had an epiphany: As long as I was working more than fifty-six hours per week, I was spending *the majority of my waking hours* at work. In other words, I was spending more than half of my life on something that I didn't really care about.

This realization presented a fork in the road: figure out how to earn enough money while working fewer hours so that I could fit more life into those extra hours; or, work on something that would be worthy of half my life. I think both options are entirely reasonable, and the path each person takes depends on their own circumstances. What was *not* reasonable for me was to continue spending half my life on something that didn't matter to me.

I decided to make a commitment that I would only work on jobs that I cared about—things that would leverage my unique superpowers (more on that shortly) to make what I would consider a positive impact on the world. I knew that would not always be possible; I may not be able to find a job that fulfilled those criteria and paid enough money.

But it's been nearly ten years and so far I haven't had to look back. I ended up quitting my Wharton MBA program before it started (sadly, after paying the nonrefundable deposit). I led startups in mental health and personal-finance education, pivoted to working at Boston College and starting the nonprofit OpenMind, before pivoting again to my current role running Dialog. Each of these transitions was born out of many considerations, but each time I honored the commitment I had made: only embark on a new job if it's something I care about.

Of course, doing so is a privilege that not everyone has—for many people, prioritizing other factors, like the needs of their family, make this commitment impossible. I certainly had a lot of luck along the way. However, I do know that *everyone* is capable of shaping their career at least a bit more in the direction of something they really want to be doing.

First (as always!), you must determine what you want. In this chapter, I'll help you figure out:

1. What do you want from your career? – Of course, this answer changes over time. Your dream career is a journey, not a destination. But the next few years are critical; if you don't commit to gathering the information you need, you run the risk of drifting along, making job decisions based on criteria you don't truly care about, and wasting half your waking life in the process.

2. How do you get it? – You'll learn about landing difficult-to-get jobs, networking (even if that word itself makes you want to vomit), and negotiating.

Unearth your superpowers

Through my work at Dialog—an under-the-radar organization that curates retreats and conversations for some of the most influential people in the world—I've observed that the most successful people in the world are not the ones who force themselves into a box of "what this job requires," nor do they force themselves to get better at the things they are not naturally good at. They are the ones who take (and shape) a role that enables them to spend as much of their time and energy as possible using their superpowers.

A superpower is something that:

1. You are better at than your peers (you're in the top 5%)
2. You like to do
3. You value getting better at (you respect someone who is really good at it)

You cannot build a fantastic career by merely smoothing over your weaknesses. Rather, you must discover your unique superpowers, and craft a career that utilizes them as much as possible. In fact, this is the other big reason I decided to pivot away from my first job in management consulting: I felt like I had spent three years getting slightly better at some of my weaknesses (including creating PowerPoint slides), and very little time working on my biggest strengths. This is often true of jobs that have "associate" or "analyst" positions, in which every newcomer must be molded to become an interchangeable cog in a machine.[50]

Discovering your superpowers is a lifelong journey filled with plenty of revisions as you learn more about yourself. But in order to start, here are some things you can start doing now:

---

50 This may be a harsh generalization; it really depends on the company, and even on who your manager is. And some weaknesses *must* be smoothed over before you can progress. For example, almost every job in the modern world requires that you have decent communication skills.

1. Feedback – Ask for it frequently, then act on it. In order to discover if you are really good at something, you need others' perspectives on your work. The more you ask for feedback, the more accurate your perception will be of your own talents.

2. Experiment – If a new project piques your interest, jump on it. The more new things you try (assuming they appeal to you in the first place), the larger your sample size will be of "skills I have tried using" to ultimately discover your superpowers.

3. Double down – If you liked doing something and did well on it, do more of it. I like to say to my employees (only half-jokingly): "Your reward for doing good work is more work." But hopefully that sounds exciting! When you do a good job on a project, ask for more projects that are like it (but even more challenging).

4. Outsource – If you didn't like doing something, get it off your plate. All jobs require doing some amount of work you don't like, because it just has to get done. But that doesn't mean that *you* always have to be the one to do it, or that you can't do it more efficiently.

If you're constantly seeking to get leverage on your time—through automating, outsourcing, or delegating—a higher and higher percentage of your daily workload will involve your superpowers (because you will be doing the things that only you can do). You can be creative about this: Does your company work with temps that you can use? Can you use Zapier or ChatGPT plugins to automate some of your workflow? Can you ask another manager to borrow 10% of an intern's time?

5. Keep track – At the end of every day, write down the tasks that drained your energy versus the tasks that gave you energy (these are typically correlated with being good at something and enjoying it). If you don't keep track, you probably won't remember them!

Not every job you have will enable you to do all of these things, but at the very least you can proactively make them a part of your PD chats with your manager.

For my team, I created a shared document called "The Hall of Superheroes." Everyone is required to update their page in the doc at least twice per year so that we have a viewable record of each person's superpowers.

As an example, here is a sampling from my own list:

- Reasoning from first principles (asking questions others don't ask)
- Super efficient (can get through a long to-do list quickly, even if it requires frequent context-switching)
- Keeping calm under pressure (making decisions rationally during crises)
- Writing emails
- Public speaking
- Having difficult conversations
- Teaching, explaining things (clearly, in a logical order)
- Challenging people (pushing them to grow)

Of course, if you are relatively early in your career you won't have as many data points to base your draft superpowers on. But as a starting point, you can do a brief reflection exercise. Go ahead and answer these questions in your notebook (right now!):

1. **What recent projects at work did you really love?**
2. **When you last received high praise, what was it for?**
3. **What accomplishments (at work, at school, or in life) are you most proud of? What skills and qualities enabled you to accomplish them?**
4. **When you leave the room, what do you hope people will say about you?**

5. **What would your biggest champion in your career say about you?**
6. **What do the people who most love you in the world love you for?**

Every three to six months, you can come back to these questions and answer them anew, then revise your list of superpowers accordingly.

The criteria that matter

Ten years ago, the criteria I committed to optimizing for myself could be evaluated via two tests:

1. The morning test – When you wake up, are you excited to go to work?
2. The nighttime test – When you are trying to fall asleep and are looking back at your past week, month, or year, do you feel like your work made a difference?

The morning test includes job factors such as hours, flexibility, pay, and coworkers. Over the course of years, it might feel like all of these pale in comparison to the nighttime test; if you look back at a career full of wasted potential, isn't it worth pushing through some of the misery? Certainly. At the same time, if you *only* prioritize the long term, it's unlikely you will be successful. Without a passion for (at least some of) what you're doing day to day, you are liable to lose your competitive edge in the long term.

One more note about fulfillment: If you have an ambitious goal for the long term, frame it as "to be doing X" rather than "to have done X." For example, instead of saying, "By the end of my career, I want to have run a large company," say, "At some point during my career, I want to be running a large company." That's because the moment of accomplishing your goal only lasts for a moment (as we learned in skill #2). The moment you became the CEO will quickly pass, and then you will be faced with the question—for many, many more moments—"Do I actually want to be doing this?" If you spend all your time trying to have done something, you won't be happy; instead, try to be satisfied with being in the act of doing it.

Here is a more complete list of the primary factors that lead to a job meeting (or failing) the two tests:

Compensation

- Salary – What is the total compensation, including the expected (average) bonus as well as stock or equity?
- Benefits – Calculate the monetary value of these and add them to the salary.

Life balance[51]

- Hours – What is the total amount of time you need to put in?
- Flexibility – Do you have the ability to shape your hours around your schedule?
- Time off – How many vacation days, holidays, sick days are offered? How much parental and medical leave?
- Location – Do you have a long commute? (More time spent commuting means less time doing other life things.) How close is it to family and friends?
- Stress – How much mind space does the job take up when you're not at work?

Daily work

- Superpowers – Do you get to lean into them?
- Responsibility – Do you get to make decisions that you care about making?
- Personal impact – Does the work you do matter (to at least one other person)?

51 Some people may choose to prioritize the criteria in this section above all others. It's possible that you find the most meaning in life from things you do outside of work (such as family or religion) and want to optimize your career to make it possible to spend more time on those things.

Growth

- Learning – Are you acquiring the skills and knowledge you need?
- Career development – Does this job help you get to your next step (sometimes through getting the right connections, or the right line on your resume)?

People

- Manager (perhaps the most important) – Are they an aid to optimizing all of the above, or an impediment?
- Coworkers – Do you like them? Are you getting to build real relationships with them?
- Culture – Do people trust each other? Is it fun?

Physical environment

- Comfort – Are you getting what you need while at work (sunlight, food, ability to sit—or stand—enough)?

Obviously, no job will be perfect along all of these dimensions. And often, two criteria are in direct opposition to each other. For example, I'm willing to take on more stress in order to have more responsibility (because worrying about work more often comes with being responsible for more people or a larger budget).

What are your criteria? Again, these will be refined over time—but as a starting point, think about your current job:

- Does it pass the morning test (when you wake up, are you excited to go to work)? (yes or no)
- Does it pass the nighttime test (when you are trying to fall asleep and looking back at your past week, month, or year, do you feel like your work made a difference)? (yes or no)

- What are your top seven criteria for a job? (Don't worry about the order, you can always reorder them later.)

In order to develop this list further, don't restrict your inputs to the things you can observe. You can benefit from other's observations as well, by . . .

Talking to other people

We are woefully unaware of what careers exist out there. The only way to learn about them—and what they are like—is through talking to people who have experienced them. I've had informal career chats with hundreds of people.

Actively seek out people who have jobs that are interesting to you (we'll discuss this aspect of networking more very soon). During your conversations with them, you'll want to ask questions to find out what they *actually* do. It often won't be what you expected. You'll also want to find out about the path they took to where they are now, in case you decide to try to get there as well.

Here are some questions I've found particularly helpful in these informal career chats, to unearth some of the less obvious insights:

- What was the most rewarding project you ever worked on? What made it fun? [To see if you have the same sense of what's rewarding and what's fun.]
- What's one thing you have to do in your current role that you hate but that's worth doing to be in this role? [To get an honest sense of the trade-offs.]
- What is one wrong decision you've made? [People tend to share only the good decisions they made—unless you ask.]
- What are the necessary skills or accomplishments you need to have to get to where you are, versus which are just "nice to have"? [People often assume that the path they took is the only way, unless you prod.]

How to get a good job in the first place

As we learned in skill #2, the only way to get something is to try! The goal is to maximize the number of goals you make, not your shots-to-goals ratio. It doesn't matter if you get rejected ninety-nine times; it only matters if you get a job you really want.

Almost everyone has dream jobs that are possible (albeit difficult) to get, but they never find out if they can because they never try.

As an exercise, try to come up with three jobs you think might be amazing and that you are at least somewhat qualified for (jobs that would be a stretch, but not totally infeasible).

There are many resources out there that can help you learn how to apply for jobs that are posted—including how to craft your resume, how to write a compelling cover letter, and how to interview well. These are certainly worth investing time in.

What I want to help you with here is how to apply for jobs that are *not* posted. Recruiters estimate that 80% of jobs are never officially posted. Rather, the company hired someone internally—or someone who proactively reached out.

There are four methods that have worked well for me:

1. Get specific – Suppose you want to work in graphic design. Spend time online to find the three top graphic-design agencies whose style resonates with you personally. Then, within each of those companies, spend time reading about the people in order to find the managers you would most want to work for. Stalk them on LinkedIn and Google if the company doesn't have lots of info posted on their website. Reach out to these people—and now you will have a great email just waiting to be written, about why you want to work for *their* firm specifically, and for *them* as a manager specifically.

2. Play the long game – Often, great people at great companies don't happen to be actively hiring right now. That doesn't matter. Unless you are desperate for a salary right now, your goal is not to get a job—your goal is to develop a relationship that will lead to a job. You can still be direct about your intentions ("I think I want to work for you one day"), but for now just aim to have a conversation and learn more about the manager and the company. That way, you won't appear desperate, which can be a turnoff.

For example, there is one seemingly incredible company I've long admired and been interested in working for someday. In my first conversation with a manager there, I asked, "What would I need in order to work for you?" He responded pretty directly, "You'd need to get some more gray hair on your head first." (In other words, be older.) It was disappointing at the time, but it's okay. I've continued to stay in touch with him—and to meet other people at the company—so that if or when the time comes, I will have a vastly greater chance of landing a role than the average candidate who is coming in cold. (I already have the opening line of my cover letter ready: "Unfortunately, I've started to bald before going gray . . .")

3. Give them something they never asked for – If you have a stellar letter of recommendation, include it in your email. Just because they didn't ask for it doesn't mean they won't value it. Even more impactful is to do some sample work for them. Of course, you don't want to go overboard (see above about appearing desperate!), and you don't want to be taken advantage of (you can set a limit in advance of how much work you're willing to do for free).

For example, I cofounded the nonprofit organization OpenMind with someone who was way out of my league, a well-known professor and author named Jonathan Haidt. I met Jonathan through a mutual connection (our third cofounder, Caroline) and pitched him the idea: I wanted to reduce political polarization by teaching college students how to have conversations with people they disagree with—and to do it at scale, via online learning. He wasn't convinced it would work, and (very nicely) rejected me. So that night, I stayed up late writing the first lesson and programming it using a basic low-code tool and sent it to him, along with a pitch deck explaining how we would further develop and disseminate it. He wrote: "I am totally blown away. I want to work with you in some way." Note that the sample work wasn't incredible (I made it in one night!), but it showed him what was possible. It's also worth noting that, at the time, he didn't have the funding to work with me, but the seed was sown—he wanted to work with me "in some way," and now the only question was *how* (which we eventually solved).

4. Build your network – It's not "cheating" to get a job through a connection. In school, you are conditioned to play a very specific kind of game. For example, you must memorize facts for a test because opening your book during the test is considered cheating. The rules of this academic game often make sense because it's designed for learning.

By contrast, when you're in the real world, the only game that is being played is the game of life, in which you can—and should—use every (reasonable and ethical) resource at your disposal to achieve your goals. Getting a job purely through "merit" (applying for an open role with a basic resume) doesn't have a different outcome than getting a job through perseverance or through a mutual connection.

So, in order to build up as many possible connections as possible, you can learn how to get good at . . .

Networking

I used to hate that word. To me, it implied wearing formal clothes and shaking lots of hands and having superficial interactions. In reality, good networking is not superficial at all—it's forming deep connections with people you find interesting. It can actually be (and I can't believe I'm writing this) really fun.

Imagine someone assigned you this project: Go find five of the most fascinating people you are connected to, then have an interesting conversation with them. That sounds fun to me! Actually, you don't need someone to assign you this project—you can do it right now. At first, the five most fascinating people you are connected to may not be CEOs and celebrities. But as you get to know them, and they introduce you to more people, the barriers between you and people you really admire will start to dissolve, because you'll build up more and more mutual connections. That's networking.

Here are some basic (fun!) principles for networking:

1. Reach out in a way that makes them want to respond – People typically want to be helpful. But they are also busy. I've found that people are most willing to take the time to help when they believe that they can make a difference. So, I try to frame my outreach this way: "In just fifteen minutes of your time, I think you can have a big impact on me." And, of course, the shorter the message, the better. Here's a template you can use:

> Barry – My name is Raffi, and I'm writing a book published by Chronicle Books based on the Adulting 101 course I created and taught at Boston College. [Introduce yourself first, and quickly share one of the most impressive things about yourself.]
>
> I heard your interview about negotiating with Auren Hoffman on his podcast, and I learned so much from you—you explain these concepts really well. [A little flattery never hurts, as long as it's sincere.] One of the topics I'm covering is negotiating, and I'd love to get your advice—I think that with just fifteen minutes of your time, you can have a major impact on the book.
>
> Are you free for a short call any time in the next few weeks? If so, feel free to send over some times that work. [Make the request specific and concrete.]

2. Ask everyone to connect you to more people – At the end of each conversation, if I found it helpful, I tell them that. Then, I ask, "Because this was so helpful, I'm guessing you know other great people I should talk to. Who are two who come to mind?" I jot down their names, then look them up, then follow up by email to ask to be introduced (including specifics of why I want to talk to them).

3. Maintain your own CRM – In business-speak, a customer relationship management system is a database of all your customers, with details you want to remember about them. Starting with your first conversation, enter them into your own personal CRM—a spreadsheet (which can be very basic) to keep track of everyone.[52] Besides basic contact info, you can include a note on what your most recent conversation was about, so that you can reference it in the future. Here's a template:

Name	Email	Phone	Mutual (who connected us)	Recent date (when we last spoke)	Notes (what we last spoke about)

When I first began my role at Dialog, I was nervous about having phone calls with members, some of whom are quite high profile. Of course, getting to talk to fascinating people is fun, but sometimes my nerves would get in the way of remembering to enjoy it. I got a lot better when I realized two things.

52 I was way too late in adopting this, and lost track of an embarrassingly high number of people I wish I would have stayed in touch with.

First, the goal of a first meeting is only to have a good conversation. Often, we meet with people from whom we want something: a job, a connection, a favor. If we come in guns blazing, we don't leave space for a genuine connection to happen. So, instead, I typically forgo my request on the first call. Sometimes we hit it off, then making the request later is easy.

Second, we often *don't* hit it off—and that's okay. I've had conversations with many Dialog members where we didn't happen to vibe. In your career, you don't need everyone to really like you. Often, the (relatively few) people who do are the people who can most help you, because they will genuinely *want* to help you.

For example: I've wanted to write this book for a long time, but I had no connections in the publishing world. One night at a Dialog retreat, I had a great conversation with a professor about my decision to have many children. Later, she reached out because she was writing a book on that topic and wanted to write about some of what I said in our conversation. Her editor read the passage and said he wanted to meet me. That editor introduced me to my agent, who found me a publisher. Looking back, I never would have expected it to happen like that! But it did, because at one fortuitous time, I was solely focused on having an interesting conversation.

How to negotiate

Barry Nalebuff, the negotiations expert (from that draft cold email earlier!), talks about how most people fundamentally misunderstand negotiating. We have a misconception that it works the way it does in movies: Someone proposes a high number, the other person counters with a low number, and they haggle back and forth in a hard-charging contest of wills. As with many topics in movies, negotiations are portrayed this way because it makes for an entertaining scene, not because it's how they work in real life.

Most negotiations are not a zero-sum game; there is no fixed-size pie that you are haggling over how to divvy up. Rather, both parties have their own constraints, and they try to find the optimal way to make it work for both of them. Thus, negotiating is often about expanding the size of the pie—working to find creative options to add to the table.

Of course, the optimal tactics for a negotiation depend on what it's for. We'll start with some principles for negotiating a raise (at a job you currently have), then for negotiating a starting salary (at a new job). For a raise:

1. Gather information – Determine how much your time is worth, at least on paper. You can ask coworkers you trust, and use websites like glassdoor.com, to find out how much people in your position (or the position above you that you are aiming to be promoted to) get paid. Likewise, find out how long it takes before others get promoted and how often they get raises.

2. Do the work for your manager – In many cases, your manager *wants* to pay you more, but they are constrained by what their boss says or by a budget they need to stick to. So, you can make your manager's job easier by writing a note they can share with their boss, or by proposing ideas for how to make room in the budget.

3. Show appreciation – Sometimes, you can negotiate by expressing discontent and threatening to quit; but often, that can backfire. Instead, it's best to share the ways in which you genuinely like your work, and what you like about your boss—and why you're excited about your future working together. That will demonstrate that you're on the same team.

4. Share why the money matters to you – This one depends on your relationship with your manager. If you feel comfortable, you can explain how a higher salary will enable you to work harder—you'll be able to afford ordering in more so you won't have to cook as much, or you can hire people to do more of your household work.

At the very least, you can share that a raise will help you feel recognized and motivate you to work even harder.

5. Demonstrate that you already have the new role – Ideally, you can show that you are already doing the work of the next level up, so getting a promotion would just formalize it on paper. One framework you can use: Show that you were mandated to do X, but that you've accomplished X + Y. For example: "My job was to increase sales by 20%, and not only did I do that, but I also helped you recruit two new people to the team."

Note that this approach will require you to track your accomplishments over time. Every time you complete a project, or notice an encouraging statistic, or receive praise, *write it down* and save it. Those notes will come in super handy when it's time for this negotiation.[53]

When you receive a job offer, you're in a bit of a different position, since you don't have concrete data to share about job performance (yet). But the same principle applies about wanting to foster a good relationship—since, if you take the job, you'll be working together.

1. Be enthusiastic – There's no need to play hard to get. Reiterate that you are really interested in this specific role at this specific company. The more positive things you can share, the more it shows that you are on the same team—that you want to make this job offer work out, not that you are just trying to squeeze more money out of them.

2. Make it clear you have the right skills – Presumably, they think you possess them, hence the job offer. Yet during the interview process, you probably learned many more details about the role, which

53 For a long time I neglected to do this, and I flubbed a raise negotiation as a result. During a review, my boss asked, "What are the main skills you have that have benefited us over the past three months?" and my mind totally went blank!

you can now use to go deeper: "It seems like it will be really important in the first two months to do X, and thankfully I've already done that in my role at Y."

3. Make it clear that you're in demand – If you have competing offers (or a counteroffer from your current employer), tell them. Or if you're in the latter stages of another interview process, even without an offer in hand, you can say that. In the past, I've said: "This is my first-choice job by far. If you are able to meet me at $X, I'll accept right away and withdraw from all my other interviews."

Note that this is very different than playing hard to get. You've already established that you like the role and you want to work together. At the same time, there's reality: You have other opportunities.

Of course, success in negotiating is never guaranteed. I operate under the mindset of "might as well try"—and as long as you're polite and positive, there isn't much to lose. In that spirit (and mostly for entertainment value), here are some of the salary negotiations that I've had:

- My first job in consulting – The starting salary was standardized for all entry-level associates. I tried nevertheless, including showing them two competing, higher offers I had, but they didn't budge. (I took the job anyway because the role was more exciting and I thought it would set me up better for the rest of my career.)
- An EdTech startup – I was first hired as a contractor, getting paid by the hour. When it came time for my two-month evaluation, they extended me a full-time offer. I told them I wanted a couple of days to think about it. (I said I was very likely to say yes; I just wanted some time because the work had been so intense the last few weeks.) A couple hours later, they called me to say that the offer was

rescinded—they felt that because I asked for time to think about it, that demonstrated a lack of commitment!

- Contracting for a nonprofit – I proposed an hourly rate that was way higher than what I thought they could pay, assuming we would then negotiate. But to my surprise, they just said "yes" immediately.
- Working at Boston College – I began as a career coach, helping students prepare for management consulting interviews. They said that in order to justify the salary I requested, they would have to give me the title of "Lecturer," and I said fine (it didn't make a difference to me). I later found out that anyone with the title of Lecturer is eligible to teach undergraduate courses, which is how I was able to pitch my Adulting 101 course!
- Running a small company – The owner proposed a starting salary that was much higher than I expected. I was really excited about the role and was about to say yes, but I decided to first ask for a salary that was 10% higher. He said yes.

SUMMARY

- **You now have two jobs: your day job, and the job of figuring out what to do with your career.**
- **You are more likely to be successful if you discover and leverage your superpowers (things that you are really good at, that you like to do, and that you value getting better at).**
- **You can evaluate a job based on whether it passes the morning test (are you excited to go to work that day?) and the nighttime test (looking back, do you feel satisfied with your impact?).**

- **The only way to learn about what other jobs you may like is to talk to lots of people; build your network by reaching out to people you find interesting (in a way they are likely to respond to) and aim to have a good conversation with them.**
- **Shoot for jobs that are not posted by building relationships early, and offering more than what they're asking for.**
- **Transform negotiations from a zero-sum game by expanding the size of the pie and demonstrating that you are on the same team.**

Homework

First, write down your draft list of superpowers. You can use your answers to the questions early in the chapter as a starting point. Aim to be comprehensive; you can always cut things later. Put it into a "living document" that you can go back to and update every three to six months as you learn more about yourself.

Second, identify five people who have really interesting jobs, and reach out to them cold (now this task *is* being assigned to you!). You can use the template from earlier in the chapter. If you don't hear back, follow up twice. Then, when you do have the conversations, you can use the questions I shared to really get to know what their work is like and if you want to aim for a career like theirs.

Extra credit: Ask for a raise! Even if it's off cycle, try to put the aforementioned negotiation techniques into practice. Might as well try and see what happens.

CONCLUSION

Skill #14

LIVE ON PURPOSE

Congratulations, you've learned a lot in this book! Unfortunately, it's all useless.

Unless . . . you act on it. Your mind will not become more of an asset to you unless you utilize the techniques we learned; your finances will not take care of themselves unless you manage them; your personal relationships will not improve unless you work on them; your career will not take off unless you build it.

Reading this book is no small feat—it is a meaningful accomplishment. It's also a *first* step. Your next project is to integrate everything you learned into your own life and put it into action.

Of course, you may have the best intentions to do so but not follow through on them. Intentionality—acting according to your intentions—is easier said than done. We often wake up with a plan for the day, or a resolution to act a certain way, only to find that we've already failed before even one hour of the day has passed. Why?

I had an epiphany about that question while reading the masterpiece *Of Human Bondage* by W. Somerset Maugham. The novel tells the story of Philip Carey from childhood through age thirty. As he grows, he faces nearly all of the challenges that we've covered: He changes careers multiple times; he gets stuck in fruitless romantic relationships; he makes bad investment decisions; he grapples with the question of what he wants out of life. (The book is one hundred years old, yet feels like it could have been written today!) Even when Philip knows what is best for him, he often does not act accordingly. He struggles to overcome his in-the-moment instincts. The title of the book refers to the philosopher Baruch Spinoza, who writes that we are frequently at risk of becoming a slave to (in "bondage" to) our emotions.

I realized: We live most of our lives on autopilot. Nearly every action we take during the course of a day, nearly every decision we make, nearly every way we react, is unconscious. We don't think about it, we just do it automatically. We often think of our brain as being the one making decisions (the "executive" in "executive function"), yet most of the time our brain is just running the autopilot that's been programmed into it.

I've found two ways to deal with autopilot:

1. Break out of it – When you are more aware (mindful), you can remind your brain to wake up. The next time someone does something that irks you, for example, you can pause your reaction, remember that you told yourself you want to be more patient, then act accordingly. Research shows that having some kind of cue (reminder) can be helpful if it's also tied to a reward. For some people, a simple sticky note on their monitor reminds them of their intentions, followed by rewarding themselves with a quick break when they follow through on it.

2. Reprogram it – You can *take advantage* of the fact that, despite your best efforts to do #1, you will likely still be on autopilot most of the time. So, program the autopilot to fly the plane where you want it to go. In other words: Build new habits.

At first, building a new habit takes a lot of effort. But eventually, the very fault in our brains that we are trying to address (that it acts according to habit) becomes our asset—once the habit is formed, we no longer need to think about it much.

As with mindfulness (#1), a lot has been written about how to form habits (#2). My favorite insight comes from the website ClearerThinking.org, which ran a study on nearly 500 people, testing more than twenty evidence-backed habit-formation techniques. They found that one in particular was by far the most effective: "Habit Reflection." It works like this:

- Identify a past habit you changed or developed successfully.
- Think about what you did to make that habit stick. Were there certain tactics you used? Certain things you said to yourself?
- Do those same things now, for the new habit you want to form.

It sounds so basic, yet so true: Different techniques work for different people, so if you can find the ones that worked for you in the past, they will likely work again.

A tale of two graduate students

Let me tell you a story about two different people . . .

The first reached her senior year of college and realized she didn't know what she wanted to do with her career. She was close with one of her professors, who told her she had a talent for academic research, and encouraged her to apply for graduate school. She did, and she was admitted. Beginning with her first day, she copied the playbook that had worked well for her in college—study hard and try to get good grades. She lived on the same autopilot. Halfway through her first year, she grew tired of researching and writing all the time; she began to experience burnout. She took to asking herself: "*Why* am I doing all this?" The constant questioning further sapped her motivation. In her second year, she dropped out—with still no career prospects to speak of.

The second spoke with many people about her career options. Ultimately, she learned about a kind of career she was interested in, and decided that grad school was the right move, because she needed the knowledge and the credential in order to get a job like that. She learned that getting good grades in certain classes, researching a specific topic, and growing close to certain professors would further that career aspiration. So she deliberately switched on her autopilot: work hard at school each day, without thinking about it too much. Every six months or so, she would check in with herself: "Is this still what I want?" And as long as the answer was yes, she would slip back into autopilot. She got her degree two years later and applied for jobs she was excited about.

As you no doubt noticed, the second person was able to align her daily actions with her long-term intentions.[54] When you can do that, you can worry about autopilot less, and even leverage it.

One common objection: "I cannot always act with intention upon what I want, because there are some things I simply *have* to do." But . . .

Do you *have* to do anything?

At a fundamental level, everything we do is because we want to; if it wasn't, we wouldn't do it! You can examine every decision and see that you have your own reasons for wanting to make it. For example:

- "I *have* to take my car to the repair shop" versus "I *choose* to take my car to the repair shop, because I want to be able to drive."

[54] It's certainly helpful to check up on those long-term intentions, but not so often that it distracts you from being able to thrive in your day-to-day life.

- "I'm *obligated* to go to work tomorrow" versus "I *choose* to go to work tomorrow, because I want to make enough money to live comfortably."
- "I *need* to do my tax returns" versus "I *choose* to do my tax returns, because I want to avoid being audited by the IRS."
- "I *can't* sleep with this person I'm attracted to, because I'm already in a relationship" versus "I *choose* not to sleep with this person I'm attracted to, because I want to not hurt my significant other."

This doesn't mean you have to be falsely cheery about doing unpleasant things; rather, it's about acknowledging that ultimately you want to do them for a reason. Within the fixed rules of your world, you are making choices that benefit you.

The more you see each of your actions as a choice, the more each of them will truly become a choice. I think that part of becoming an adult is eliminating the words "have to" and "need to" from your vocabulary.

And while we're on the topic of words to eliminate from your vocabulary . . . "deserve" is the worst offender! You don't "deserve" anything. You can *want* certain things, and you can avoid the people who don't help you get them—but, as we learned in skill #9 (about assertiveness), that's different from *expecting* people to grant you what you want.

Using the word "deserve" in your self-talk is a trap, in both directions:

- "I don't deserve this much" – If you think you deserve too little, you will turn down good opportunities.
- "I deserve to get what I want" – If you think you deserve too much, you are setting yourself up for disappointment. (No one "owes" you anything, even love—they *choose* to love you. Grant other people the sense of agency that you now give yourself!)

Parting words

Of course, acting according to your intentions yields the best returns when you have the right intentions. Which brings us to our original question from skill #1 . . . what do you want?

To recap briefly: As you get older, you have more freedom but also more responsibility—including responsibility for your own LTF (long-term fulfillment). As a kid, you could drift along, because if you had good parents, they would be the ones worrying about your happiness. But as an adult, if you aren't careful, you'll let your life be determined by things your parents previously said, or your boss's expectations, or your peers' opinions. You now have "edit" access to the Google Doc of your deepest wants.

This book covered most of the important dimensions in that Google Doc. But, of course, there were many topics I did not have the space to cover, such as homeownership, taking care of your body, becoming a parent, facing the loss of loved ones, and more.

Also, while we consistently emphasized your growth into Stage 4 of adult development (self-authorship), we did not address how to get to Stage 5 (the self-transforming mind). Adulthood itself is not an achievement or a destination to be arrived at; it is a lifelong endeavor. Being "self-transforming" is about embracing the changes that inevitably occur and incorporating them into your life intentionally.

And that is only one framework among many that describes the ways in which you can continue to grow as an adult, well into your thirties, forties, fifties, and beyond . . . For now, I will leave you with the bittersweet taste of mystery on your lips.

The adult world is full of these mysteries to explore and new ideas to discover. You will face challenges, but you are strong. *You* are the one who controls your fate. You are no longer living your life by accident; you are living life on purpose.

SUMMARY

- What you learned in this book is useless unless you act on it.
- Intentionality (acting according to our intentions) can be difficult because we mostly run on autopilot; we can address that by (1) setting reminders to snap out of autopilot (mindfulness), and (2) reprogramming our autopilot (forming habits).
- You don't "have" to do anything, and you don't "deserve" anything; when you live life on purpose, everything you do is ultimately because you want to.

That was a summary of this chapter, but what about the whole book? Here is my best attempt at summarizing the main takeaway from each chapter:

1. Determine for yourself "what are the purposes of my life right now?"
2. Treasure your rejections, because they make you unafraid of trying new things.
3. Question everything you hear and read (including this book).
4. Reframe your overly negative automatic thoughts into more realistic thoughts.
5. Build your credit by utilizing a credit card, and paying it back in full each month.
6. Invest your 401(k) and IRA in an S&P 500 index fund, in order to afford retirement.
7. Get enough car insurance and health insurance to cover (at the very least) any serious liability you could incur; file your tax return (form 1040) each year before April.
8. Build your budget and update it over time to keep it realistic.

9. Be assertive (unafraid to state your needs) and approach disagreements with curiosity.
10. Approach dating like a treasure hunt, then actively work on becoming a better partner.
11. Express gratitude to your parents without always doing what they want.
12. Make your manager's life as easy as possible.
13. Identify your career superpowers and talk to many people about what they do.
14. Reprogram your autopilot so that you can live life on purpose.

This is a very broad summary. Hopefully, having read the chapters, you understand the reasoning for and nuance behind each conclusion. There's no shame in going back (multiple times) to review any of this material!

Homework

In the Adulting 101 class that I taught, the students had lots of homework each week: They not only did the real-life tasks, but also reflected on them, wrote about them, read books, and (at the end of the year) wrote their own comprehensive "adulting plan." Unfortunately, one of the limits of the medium I have been using to communicate with you (a book) is that I cannot enforce the homework!

Given what you read in this chapter, I hope you understand the importance of the homework tasks to make all this worthwhile. If you have not yet done the homework from all the other chapters, this is your assignment: Go back and pick the one that you think is most important. Do it now.

Extra credit: Of course, there's not actually such a thing as "extra credit." You certainly shouldn't do anything just to please me—nor because you're "supposed" to. You should only do what benefits your LTF!

However, assuming you find this extra credit assignment to be aligned with your goals . . . I suggest doing what I mentioned in skill #2 to celebrate a milestone: "Set up camp for the night." In other words, celebrate with your friends the milestone of having finished this book! Take them out to dinner (assuming it's within your budget[55]), and share one or two of the most impactful things you've learned.

55 Sorry, I couldn't resist.

Recommended Reading and Viewing

If you would like to dive deeper into some of the topics we covered, here are my top book, blog, and film recommendations:

Skill #3:
The Cook and the Chef by Tim Urban (blog piece)

Skill #4:
Feeling Good by David Burns

Skill #6:
A Random Walk Down Wall Street by Burton Malkiel

Skill #9:
How to Win Friends and Influence People by Dale Carnegie

Skill #11:
Guess Who's Coming to Dinner (movie)

Skill #13:
The Defining Decade by Meg Jay (also relevant to skill #10)

Skill #14:
The Magicians by Lev Grossman (novel)
Of Human Bondage by W. Somerset Maugham (novel)

Acknowledgments

First of all, a big thanks to you, the reader, for diligently absorbing the material in this book, without taking a frivolous break to read its Acknowledgments section . . . right? (Get back to reading!)

As with any major endeavor, this book would not have come into being without a long sequence of contributions by wonderful people . . .[56]

- If my parents, **Monica** and **Joel Grinberg**, had never had me, I would not have existed, and never would have met . . .
- **Amy Donegan**, who hired me at Boston College, and supported my idea to create and teach an "Adulting 101" course, during which time I met . . .
- Mentors **Jonathan Haidt** and **Auren Hoffman**, each of whom once hired me for an exciting job I wasn't quite qualified for, but believed in me and in our shared ambition, through which I met . . .
- **Doriane Coleman**, with whom I had a fascinating conversation, which led to more conversations, after which she graciously introduced me to her literary agent . . .
- **Jim Levine**, who became my agent as well, and who saw potential in this atypical idea, eventually bringing it to . . .
- **Cara Bedick**, my first editor at Chronicle Books, who understood the vision for a book about adulting skills, and **Maddy Wong**, my second editor, who spent many hours bringing us to the finish line.

I am grateful for the time and insightful contributions of my earliest readers. These include the subject-matter experts who reviewed each chapter in detail:

[56] I'm taking my own advice about how to write emails, and putting this in bullet point form to save you time.

- **Jennifer Garvey Berger** (adult development)
- **Tim Urban, John Townsend, Kaja Perina** (mental skills)
- **Kevin Brennan, Barry Nalebuff, Ken Broad, Mark Colodny** (financial skills)
- **David McRaney, Stephanie Kaplan Lewis, Meg Jay, Sara Kuburic** (relationship skills)
- **Srishti Gupta** (career skills)
- **Charles Duhigg** (habits)

Each of them is a brilliant person whose work I admire, and it was a privilege to have their minds shaping my work.

Early readers also include the twentysomethings who provided valuable feedback from the perspective of a target reader:

- **Katie Smith, Mike Byrne, Courtney Paganelli** from the Levine Greenberg Rostan agency
- My former student **Danielle Delay**
- My former colleagues **Annabel Ostrow, Rachel Picket,** and **Aria Babu**

I have immense gratitude for the longtime support of my brother **Josh Grinberg** and sister-in-law **Goldie Grinberg**, my best friends/ next-door neighbors **Daniel Gastfriend** and **Julie Shain**, as well as **Jonathan Cohen** and the entire Gann "Justice League of Friends" (for twenty years and counting).

I am also grateful to the many people who make my daily life possible. These include my employees at Dialog, especially the team leads who do incredible work and make working together a joy: **Kristin Cameron**, **Amanda Harter**, **Juliette Levine**, and **Mike San Marzano** (each of whom has, I'm told, a cardboard cutout of me on their desk). Also the wonderful nanny who takes care of the kids and enables our household to function: **Yeethiopia Tadesse**.

Said household would be a lot less full of energy, laughter, and beautiful chaos if it weren't for my children: **Judah**, **Nelida**, **Dalia**, **Gideon**, and **Carmelle**. (I can't say they helped write this book, but I can say that they often came to my computer while it was off, clacked on the keyboard, and declared, "Look at me, I'm working!")

And finally, to the one who makes everything possible for me, who makes my life as happy as it is, who is the love of my life . . . this book will end where it began—where my adult life begins and ends—with **Charlotte**.

Contact

You can follow my current writing at raffigrinberg.com. There, you can also find a link to join an online community of like-minded readers.

I keep in touch with many former students, and I love to hear from new ones. If you have a question about something in this book—or about something we didn't cover, or a relevant dilemma in your own life—feel free to reach out. You can email me at author@raffigrinberg.com.

I can't promise I'll be able to get back to you, although I do strive to reply and sometimes feature responses to FAQs in my online writing. (If you don't hear back from me, don't let the rejection get to you! Follow-up is key.)

About the Author

Raffi Grinberg is a business leader, author, and educator based in Washington, DC. He created and taught the popular Adulting 101 course at Boston College. He runs Dialog and cofounded the Constructive Dialogue Institute (with Jonathan Haidt), both multimillion-dollar organizations. He graduated with honors from Princeton University and previously worked in management at Bain & Company. He is the author of a mathematics textbook published by Princeton University Press. There's more, but . . . his bio is much less important than *your* bio, which this book will help you shape.

Library of Congress Cataloging-in-Publication Data available.

ISBN 978-1-7972-3107-5

Manufactured in China.

Design by Paul Wagner.
Infographics by Ben English.
Typeset in Grenette Pro and Neue Haas Grotesk.

10 9 8 7 6 5 4 3 2 1

CHRONICLE PRISM

Chronicle Prism is an imprint of Chronicle Books LLC,
680 Second Street, San Francisco, California 94107

www.chronicleprism.com